The
Millennium

The
Millennium

A Journey through the Sabbath of Time

by

Phyllis Carol Olive

BONNEVILLE BOOKS

Springville, Utah

ISBN: 1-55517-661-5
e.1

Published by Bonneville Books
An imprint of Cedar Fort, Inc.
925 N. Main Springville, Utah, 84663
www.cedarfort.com

Distributed by:

Typeset by Marny K. Parkin
Cover design by Adam Ford
Cover design © 2002 by Lyle Mortimer
Printed in the United States of America
10 9 8 7 6 5 4 3 2 1
Printed on acid-free paper

Library of Congress Cataloging-in-Publication Data

Olive, Phyllis Carol.
    The millennium : a journey through the Sabbath of time / by Phyllis Carol Olive.
        p. cm.
    Includes bibliographical references.
    ISBN 1-55517-661-5 (pbk. : alk. paper)
    1. Second Advent. 2. Millennialism. 3. Church of Jesus Christ of Latter-day Saints--Doctrines.   I. Title.
BX8643.S43O45 2002
236'.9--dc21
                                                            2002008045

Contents

Preface

Little doubt remains in the hearts of anyone anymore that the Millennium is near. But because of Lucifer's incessant attacks upon the righteous and the darkness which now engulfs the world, our vision of that glorious time has dimmed somewhat and needs to be refreshed. Unfortunately, it is difficult to think of the future when the present is filled with despair. But it is precisely because of our current condition that we must restore our vision of tomorrow and renew our determination to stand fast in these turbulent times, confident in the knowledge that Christ will soon be coming to sweep the wicked away and to usher in his glorious millennial reign.

These last days are both great and terrible. Although wickedness is rampant, never before in the history of the world has mankind enjoyed such wonders and miracles as do those of us in these latter days. Science and technology have literally revolutionized the way we live. We can speak with others around the world in an instant or fly to any given destination in relative ease and comfort. Our modern day computers have brought the world into our homes and the outer reaches of space into view. Medicine has progressed to the point where we can receive new hearts or limbs and a new hope for survival that seemed impossible just a short time ago. Yet there is still more to learn and discover than we can even imagine—knowledge that will freely be given during the great day of the Lord.

> And to them will I reveal all mysteries, yea, all the hidden mysteries of my kingdom from days of old, and for ages to come, will I make known unto them. . . .
>
> Yea, even the wonders of eternity shall they know, and things to come will I show them, even the things of many generations.
>
> And their wisdom shall be great, and their understanding reach to heaven; . . .
>
> For by my Spirit will I enlighten them, and by my power will I make known unto them the secrets of my will—yea, even those things which eye has not seen, nor ear heard, nor yet entered into the heart of man. (D&C 76:7–10)

Such great things are in store for the millennial man and woman that nothing we could sacrifice would be considered too great to be a part of that glorious time.

The winding up scene of this earth's telestial condition is frightening indeed, but the great millennial day which follows will be so glorious and wonderful that those who have a clear picture of it in their mind's eye will be willing to endure whatever is needed to be a part of that Zion-oriented society. Unfortunately, Satan has veiled the earth in such darkness that we sometimes need reminding that the Millennium is at our very doors and soon the earth and all her righteous inhabitants will enjoy a Sabbath of peace. This work is designed to renew that vision.

Chapter One

In the Beginning

*For in the beginning was the Word, even the Son,
who is made flesh, and sent unto us by the will of the
Father. (JST John 1:16)*

In the beginning, God created the heavens and the earth
and everything in them. By the power of his Word were they
created, for: "In the beginning was the Word, and the Word
was with God, and the Word was God. . . . All things were
made by him; and without him was not any thing made that
was made" (John 1:1–3).

By his very command the heavens and the earth came
into existence. He said, "Let there be light," and it was so. He
said, "Let the waters be gathered together into one place and
let dry land appear" and it was so. At his command two great
lights appeared, one to rule the day and the other to rule the
night and he set them in the firmament to give light to the earth
and to govern its times and seasons. By the same process he
created great oceans and seas as well as fresh water pools,
lakes and streams. He commanded the earth to bring forth
grass, herbs, and a variety of brush and fruit bearing trees and
it was even as he spake it. He then created untold varieties of
wildlife and all the organisms necessary to sustain our planet.
Then, as the crowning jewel of all creation, God created man
and woman. He commanded them to go forth and to fill up
the earth, to subdue the land, and to work out their salvation

(Moses 2:1-31). And on the seventh day he rested from his labors (Moses 3:2).

Our valiant Mother Earth was designed to be home to mortal man for the space of seven millenniums (D&C 77:6). Six of those periods would be set aside for man to experience the effects of good and evil, to be tempted by the devil and to learn to discern between his evil influence and the power of the Almighty who rains down gifts and blessings upon all those who love him and keep his commandments. The seventh period would be a time of rest, a millennium of spiritual renewal and peace.

~ ~ ~

The earth was created as a proving ground, a place where we, as Father's spirit children, could take upon ourselves a body of flesh and blood and to be acted upon by the forces of both good and evil, and, by our God-given agency, choose either the one or the other. For eons we were nurtured by his side. The time eventually came, however, for us to leave his presence and be tried and tested—to prove our integrity, to test our character and to see if we would make right choices, even in the face of impossible odds. Those who did so were promised the greatest of all rewards—that of exaltation (Moses 1:39). Lesser kingdoms would be provided for those who missed the mark. Thus, a conversation ensued about the matter, and one among them said:

> And there stood one among them that was like unto God, and he said unto those who were with him: We will go down, for there is space there, and we will take of these materials, and we will make an earth whereon these may dwell;
>
> And we will prove them herewith, to see if they will do all things whatsoever the Lord their God shall command them;
>
> And they who keep their first estate shall be added upon; and they who keep not their first estate shall not have glory in the same kingdom with those who keep their first

estate; and they who keep their second estate shall have
glory added upon their heads for ever and ever. (Abr. 3:24–26)

When all was said and done, a grand council was called
and the Father's plan presented to his spirit offspring. Tragically, a third part rejected it in favor of a plan designed by
Lucifer, a son of the morning (D&C 29:36). But the greater
numbers shouted for joy at the prospect, for with the Father's
plan, those who endured well would be exalted and privileged
to live with him forever.

For behold, this is my work and my glory—to bring
to pass the immortality and eternal life of man. (Moses 1:39)

Each and every spirit who attended that pre-mortal council was fully informed of just how difficult mortality would be.
But the rewards for the faithful were so great and so monumental in scope that they were willing to endure whatever was
needed to attain them. Thus, the Father's plan, with Jesus as
the advocate, was accepted and those series of commands
given that began the process of bringing our earth into existence.

~ ~ ~

Now because Lucifer's plan was not accepted by the
majority and, thus, rejected in the Grand Council in Heaven,
he and his followers rebelled. Such rebellion had immediate
and eternal consequences, and they were cast out of heaven—
never to receive the rewards of the just.

And the great dragon was cast out, that old serpent,
called the Devil, and Satan, which deceiveth the whole
world: he was cast out into the earth, and his angels were
cast out with him. (Rev. 12:9)

They were consigned to the earth in their spirit forms to
act as tempters, and thus further God's work of testing and trying the remainder of his children.

> And it must needs be that the devil should tempt the
> children of men, or they could not be agents unto them-
> selves; for if they never should have bitter they could not
> know the sweet. (D&C 29:39)

Lucifer did not go quietly, however, and vowed in his
anger to draw away as many of his spirit brothers and sisters
as possible, and thus thwart God's efforts to exalt them. Consequently, the war for the souls of men began.

In speaking to Moses shortly after Lucifer appeared to
him, the Lord informed Moses of that old serpent's diabolical
plot to lead men down to hell.

> And I, the Lord God, spake unto Moses, saying: That
> Satan, whom thou hast commanded in the name of mine
> Only Begotten, is the same which was from the beginning,
> and he came before me, saying—Behold, here am I, send
> me, I will be thy son, and I will redeem all mankind, that
> one soul shall not be lost, and surely I will do it; wherefore
> give me thine honor.
>
> But, behold, my Beloved Son, which was my Beloved
> and Chosen from the beginning, said unto me—Father, thy
> will be done, and the glory be thine forever.
>
> Wherefore, because that Satan rebelled against me,
> and sought to destroy the agency of man, which I, the Lord
> God, had given him, and also, that I should give unto him
> mine own power; by the power of mine Only Begotten,
> I caused that he should be cast down;
>
> And he became Satan, yea, even the devil, the father
> of all lies, to deceive and to blind men, and to lead them
> captive at his will, even as many as would not hearken unto
> my voice. . . .
>
> . . . For he knew not the mind of God, wherefore he
> sought to destroy the world. (Moses 4:1–4, 6)

It did not take Lucifer long to begin his war upon the
inhabitants of the newly formed earth. He used every scheme at
his command to corrupt the hearts of men. Adam and Eve
began to till the earth and raise up families to the Lord. Yet,

because of the evil designs of Satan and his powerful influence upon the minds of men, it was not long before there was a slow but steady decline in the more noble characteristics imparted by Adam to his posterity and a rise in depravity and sin. It pained Heavenly Father greatly to witness his children fall victim to Lucifer who by now had veiled the earth in such darkness that they were consumed in wickedness both day and night. Thus, in spite of the teachings of their great family patriarchs and those prophets who cried repentance, it took only two thousand years for Lucifer to turn their faces completely away from God and leave them ripe for destruction.

> And he beheld Satan; and he had a great chain in his hand, and it veiled the whole face of the earth with darkness; and he looked up and laughed, and his angels rejoiced. (Moses 7:26)

Nothing could save the children of Adam at this point. They had procrastinated the day of their repentance far too long and it was now everlastingly too late, and Satan knew it. Thus, in spite of the heartache involved, God gathered and directed the last few righteous among them to the City of Enoch and then carried them up and away from the earth as he unleashed the rains upon those who had so willingly forsaken him (Moses 7:69). How the heavens must have mourned as the wicked were totally and completely wiped away in a catastrophic world wide flood.

Enoch was permitted to witness that scene in vision, and noted the heavens were weeping for them in spite of their gross behavior. Enoch asked, "How is it that the heavens weep, and shed forth their tears as the rain upon the mountains?" (Moses 7:29) And God replied:

> The Lord said unto Enoch: Behold these thy brethren; they are the workmanship of mine own hands, and I gave unto them their knowledge, in the day I created them; and in the Garden of Eden, gave I unto man his agency;

5

And unto thy brethren have I said, and also given
commandment, that they should love one another, and that
they should choose me, their Father; but behold, they are
without affection, and they hate their own blood;

And the fire of mine indignation is kindled against
them; and in my hot displeasure will I send in the floods
upon them, for my fierce anger is kindled against them.

Behold, I am God; Man of Holiness is my name; Man
of Counsel is my name; and Endless and Eternal is my
name, also.

Wherefore, I can stretch forth mine hands and hold all
the creations which I have made; and mine eye can pierce
them also, and among all the workmanship of mine hands
there has not been so great wickedness as among thy brethren.

But behold, their sins shall be upon the heads of their
fathers; Satan shall be their father, and misery shall be their
doom; and the whole heavens shall weep over them, even
all the workmanship of mine hands; wherefore should not
the heavens weep, seeing these shall suffer? (Moses 7:32–37)

How tragic, yet how enlightening, that God, who had
given them so much, even the promise of exaltation, should
weep over those who had turned from him so completely.
There can be no doubt that God loves his children, even the
wayward ones. But sadly, all too many of that generation
chose to follow Lucifer instead. Thus, the rains began to fall
and continued until the waters covered the entire earth and
every living thing upon it drowned—all save Noah and his
family and those animals safely enclosed within the Ark.

~ ~ ~

Now, the great Elohim had many more spirit children
who desired the privilege of entering mortality. Thus, when
the waters subsided from off the face of the earth and it was
cleansed of those who had defiled it, life began again. But, true
to his promise to thwart God's efforts to lead his children
home, Satan immediately began to tempt the children of Noah

and their growing posterity. Thus God, in his efforts to preserve his little flock, divided the land and planted and transplanted his children in various parts of the vineyard, for had they all remained in one body the wicked might have overpowered the righteous and spoiled the whole vineyard again. In spite of such care, not many years passed before Satan had them in his clutches again, and the habitants of the earth have been spiraling downhill ever since. It is no wonder the righteous cry out for the end of it all, and plead for the time when the wicked will be destroyed and the long awaited Millennium will finally be ushered in.

~ ~ ~

Our valiant Mother Earth also yearns for that time of refreshing. In spite of the gross behavior of her children, she herself remained faithful and obedient to her Creator, giving forth her bounties at his command or withholding them when instructed (D&C 88:25–26). Therefore she, too, longs for escape. In fact, wickedness polluted her for so long that at one point she was heard to cry out, "When shall I rest?"

> And it came to pass that Enoch looked upon the earth and he heard a voice from the bowels thereof saying: Wo, Wo is me, the mother of men, I am pained, I am weary, because of the wickedness of my children. When shall I rest, and be cleansed from the filthiness which is gone forth out of me? When will my Creator sanctify me, that I may rest, and righteousness for a season abide upon my face?
>
> And when Enoch heard the earth mourn, he wept, and cried unto the Lord, saying: O Lord, wilt thou not have compassion upon the earth? Wilt thou not bless the children of Noah? (Moses 7:48–49)

A dialogue then opened up between Enoch and the Lord, and he was taught many things, including the day when the Son of God would come into the world and later be lifted up upon the cross. Once again Enoch heard the earth groan under the weight of that awful occasion, and once again he cried out, "When will the earth rest?" At long last the answer came.

> And the Lord said unto Enoch; As I live, even so will I come in the last days, in the days of wickedness and vengeance, to fulfill the oath concerning the children of Noah. And the day shall come that the earth shall rest, but before that day the heavens shall be darkened, and a veil of darkness shall cover the earth; and the heavens shall shake, and also the earth, and great tribulations shall be among the children of men, but my people will I preserve.
>
> And righteousness will I send down out of heaven; and truth will I send forth out of the earth, to bear testimony of Mine Only Begotten; His resurrection from the dead; yea and also the resurrection of all men; and righteousness and truth will I cause to sweep the earth as with a flood, to gather out mine elect from the four quarters of the earth, unto a place which I shall prepare, an Holy City, that my people may gird up their loins, and be looking forth for the time of my coming: for there shall be my tabernacle, and it shall be called Zion, a New Jerusalem.
>
> And the Lord said unto Enoch: Then shalt thou and all thy city meet them there, and we will receive them into our bosom, and they shall see us; and we will fall upon their necks, and they shall fall upon our necks, and we will kiss each other.
>
> And there shall be Mine Abode, and it shall be Zion, which shall come forth out of all the creations which I have made; and for the space of a thousand years the earth shall rest.
>
> And it came to pass that Enoch saw the day of the coming of the Son of Man, in the last days, to dwell on the earth in righteousness for the space of a thousand years. (Moses 7:60–65)

Thus, we learn that only after much tribulation and a final fiery blast of cleansing will Mother Earth be able to rest along with all those who remain faithful to their principles and keep Lucifer at bay. Sadly, their numbers will be far fewer than those who will ultimately be destroyed by the wrath of the Almighty when he descends upon the wicked at the appointed hour.

~   ~   ~

And what of our generation? Are we faring any better than those who were destroyed by the flood? Every indication points to the fact that those of our day are every bit as wicked as those who lived during the days of Noah. Moreover, because so little time is left in the war between good and evil, Satan has escalated his efforts to drag as many souls into hell as he can before his time is up. Although unseen by human eyes, his influence is greater than we know, and if we fail to put on the full armor of righteousness and live by every word that proceeds forth from the mouth of God, those of us in these latter-days are in as much peril of destruction as those who lived during the days of Noah.

Satan is waging a war of unprecedented aggression for the souls of the last few righteous upon the earth. Never before in the history of the world have the dark hosts of hell banned together with such strength and determination to lead mankind unto the mists of darkness and away from God as they have today. They hover over the nations like great billowing clouds, raining down despair, destruction, and chaos in a world struggling to survive. The ever widening influence of Satan is spreading across the nations like a plague, and his false prophets are filling the hearts of men with doctrines that please the mind yet offer only damnation for the soul. We seem helpless before him as he sweeps across the nations reaping his harvest of unclean souls. Yet it is in this very setting of anxiety and foreboding that we must look to God and to the promises given, which teach that the hope of tomorrow rests with the righteous and that the dawn of a new age is not too far distant.

Never have the Saints needed to be more steadfast in the faith than during these final years of tribulation. Thus, we must listen intently to the promptings of the Spirit and to the counsel of the leaders of the Church, and prepare ourselves in every needful thing if we are to escape the devil's design for our capture. It is for that very reason that the prophets have filled the scriptures with guidance for our day, that those of us in these latter times might better understand God's dealings with his children and Lucifer's diabolical schemes for our destruction.

> What then is the mission of Satan, that common foe of all the children of men? It is to destroy and make desolate.[1]

Lucifer is running rampant in the land. Thus we must be constantly on guard against his plan for our souls and the downfall of our country—indeed the world. Fighting him can only be done on a personal basis, however. This is a one-on-one war. But, it will be the combined efforts of many that will eventually defeat him. Brigham Young taught:

> You are aware that many think that the Devil has rule and power over both body and Spirit. Now, I want to tell you that he does not hold any power over man, only so far as the body overcomes the Spirit that is in a man, through yielding to the spirit of evil. The Spirit that the Lord puts into a tabernacle of flesh, is under the dictation of the Lord Almighty; but the spirit and body are united in order that the spirit may have a tabernacle, and be exalted; and the spirit is influenced by the body, and the body by the spirit.
>
> In the first place, the spirit is pure, and under the special control and influence of the Lord, but the body is of the earth, and is subject to the power of the Devil, and is under the influence of that fallen nature that is of the earth. If the spirit yields to the body, the Devil then has power to overcome the body and spirit of that man, and he loses both.
>
> Recollect, brethren and sisters, every one of you, that when evil is suggested to you, when it arises in your hearts, it is through the temporal organization. When you are tempted, buffeted, and step out of the way inadvertently; when you are overtaken in a fault, or commit an overt act

unthinkingly; when you are full of evil passion, and wish to yield to it, then stop and let the spirit, which God has put into your tabernacles, take the lead. If you do that, I will promise that you will overcome all evil, and obtain eternal lives. But many, very many, let the spirit yield to the body, and are overcome and destroyed.[2]

Because of the eternal nature of agency, God can only do so much to save his wayward children, for it was given them to act for themselves whether to choose good or evil. Morever, this was part of their mortal schooling. Sadly, all too many have chosen the easier way and have succumbed to every delight Satan has to offer. Once again, Satan is rejoicing over his success rate just as he did in the days of Noah. But because Christianity has also flourished over the years, it has taken him twice as long to corrupt the world this time. Yet, corrupt it he has—so much so, that with the passing of the last four thousand years, the earth is once again ripe for destruction. Things will be different this time, however, for when the earth is burned and the wicked destroyed, the righteous will inherit the earth and enjoy a millennium of peace—a time far different and far more glorious than anything we can image. Elder Bruce R. McConkie taught:

> Our mortal experiences and our finite logic—devoid of divine guidance, and without revelation from on high—would lead us to assume that life has always been as it now is, and that all things will continue everlastingly as they now are. But such is far from the fact as heaven is from hell. Neither the earth, nor man, nor life of all sorts and kinds, has always been as it now is. Mortality is but a slight and passing phase of existence, a shimmering moonbeam that shines for a moment in the darkness of our earthbound life; it is but a day in an endless eternity; something else came before, and an entirely different way of life will follow after.[3]

So great will be that time, that a prevailing spirit of peace will encompass the entire world, and the tears so commonplace in this life will be a thing of the past. Lucifer, will be chained and cast into a pit, and love will at long last be the driving force among men.

It is difficult for us to imagine life without the afflictions of sickness or pain. Neither can we truly imagine life with no crime or evil thinking or cities that shine with the presence of the Savior. All we can do in our present state is to gain a *sense* of its magnificence and set our feet on a course that will allow us entrance into that holy society.

~ ~ ~

Notes

1. Brigham Young, *Journal of Discourses*, 11:240.
2. Ibid., 2:255–56.
3. McConkie, *Millennial Messiah*, 641.

Chapter Two

The Gates of Hell
Shall Not Prevail

And again I say unto you, if ye observe to do
whatsoever I command you, I, the Lord, will turn away
all wrath and indignation from you, and the gates of
hell shall not prevail against you. (D&C 98:22)

Although the long anticipated Millennium is growing
closer every day, far too many prophecies are yet to be fulfilled for the righteous to relax their guard against the adversary and his incessant attacks upon them. His days are
numbered, but that very fact has only intensified his efforts to
drive a wedge between God and his children and to lead them
down to hell. While his diabolical plots against humanity are
centered largely in our homes, he is waging war against our
city, state, and national governments as well, and is using
every tactic at his command to bring the entire world into submission. Thus, the war between good and evil is not winding
down as the Millennium nears, but is escalating at an alarming
rate, and the righteous have never been in more peril from his
evil influence than they are today.

As hard as we try to dismiss the news of wars and those
scenes of corruption that parade before us daily on our televi-
sions, in the newspapers and even in our neighborhoods, we
cannot get away from them. The world is in such chaos that it

is becoming increasingly difficult to remain calm. Our fears and anxieties are growing stronger with the passing of each day as we watch Satan's insidious assaults upon the very principles which knit a happy, prosperous and civilized society together. Our only solace comes from the scriptures which teach that the hope of tomorrow rests with the righteous and that the dawn of a new day is not too far distant.

Many stories in the scriptures reveal mankind at their worst, or even sadder, the fact that whole civilizations turned from God at some point in their history. Yet, we must not forget that millions of God's children were born during the various ages of man and lived out their days honorably. They will thus receive the rewards of the just—even those who have never heard the gospel, for such blessings will not be withheld from them simply because of their mortal circumstances. There will be learning yet to come on the other side.

Satan, on the other hand, would have us believe men are weak or unworthy of God's love or blessings, and that only a select few will make it back into his presence. He uses discouragement, despair and depression more than any other tool at his command to lead men into darkness where he can manipulate them more easily.

Next to depression comes fear and anxiety, for the righteous know full well that many good and honorable people have suffered a variety of injustices at the hands of those under Lucifer's influence, and knowing Satan's sole purpose on earth is to destroy and to lay waste does not help the matter. There is little safety anywhere anymore, not from danger nor from sorrow nor from the evil thinking men and women who have already succumbed to Lucifer's wiles.

Yet, Biblical stories are replete with messages of hope for the righteous. The problem lies in the fact that all too often the righteous do not seem to remain righteous for long, and once they turn to wickedness the Lord must often step back and allow their enemies to destroy them. Thus, only those who remain steadfast, in spite of Satan's buffetings, will be afforded the protection of God.

Without doubt that there are hard times ahead, yet our hearts need not fail us if we remain faithful to God and to those principles of righteousness which have been given each generation of man since the beginning of time. Thus, it is imperative that we learn what our duties are to God and how to implement them in our lives. No schoolmaster can shed more light on that subject than the scriptures. Not only do they impart great spiritual truths, but historical facts as well, which often provide the lessons needed to help keep our spiritual sights in focus.

The first thousand years began with Adam, Eve and their posterity living out their days in a glorious new world. Unfortunately, Satan entered the picture immediately, and began the systematic project of corrupting the hearts of men. Thus, by the end of the second thousand years, the inhabitants of the earth were so wicked the Lord was forced to destroy them all in a catastrophic world wide flood, lest future generations be lost as well.

The third thousand years gave us the grand old patriarch Abraham. Because of his righteousness and uncompromising faithfulness he was privileged to walk and talk with God, and was promised that through his loins all the people of the earth would be blessed. Such blessings would ultimately come through his twelve great-grandsons, whose children would later be known as the Twelve Tribes of Israel.

The fourth millennium witnessed those twelve tribes grow to be a mighty nation during their bondage to Pharaoh. It also witnessed their miraculous exodus under the direction of the prophet Moses, and, because of wickedness, their ultimate dispersal throughout the world.

The fifth millennium brought with it the greatest story ever told—the life, death, and resurrection of our Lord and Savior, Jesus Christ. With his death, and that of his apostles,

15

the world was plunged into a period of darkness for a time because the light of Christ was withdrawn, a time often referred to as the Dark Ages.

Things began to turn around again during the sixth period as the Lord prepared men's hearts for the restoration of all things. Art, music, and learning flourished and discoveries of all kinds were made. Then, when the scene was set, the restoration began, including the beginning of the long awaited gathering of Israel from the four corners of the world.

Now, each of these eras experienced both highs and lows. For example, during Adam day, his posterity enjoyed the fruits of a glorious new world, yet death by murder was introduced when Cain slew Abel (Gen. 4:8). The great prophet Abraham enjoyed such spiritual maturity that he was privileged to visit with the Savior and saw the universe in vision (Abr. 3). But, in spite of his own righteousness, his posterity ultimately became so wicked the Lord had to disperse them throughout the world to preserve them from utter destruction. During the fifth millennium, the life of Jesus brought new hope to the world, but the wicked of that generation crucified him. And the restoration of the gospel in the latter times brought with it the promise of untold blessings for the righteous, yet met with opposition right from the start. But ultimately good will win out over evil, for the war for the souls of men is nearing its end with Christ coming out the victor.

~ ~ ~

While things often only *seem* darkest before the dawn, in this instance they are. Thus, we cannot help but feel a certain amount of foreboding about the coming storms, for many good people have endured much persecution in the cause of righteousness, and some have even perished. Reflections upon such incidents cannot help but cause fear and trembling in the hearts of the meek. But we must not forget that fear is a powerful weapon of the devil. It often causes the righteous to retreat rather than move forward along the narrow path which leads to life eternal. Some give up completely in the face of trouble or persecution. Some even leave the fold, which is just as Satan wants it. Unfortunately, many do not understand just how much they are giving up.

Those who lose their lives while holding fast to righteous principles will sit down in the mansions above with numerous other martyrs who loved God more than life. How our hearts mourn for the loss of the righteous under such terrible circumstances. Yet, it is their very deaths which seal the fate of the wicked and call down the fierce anger of the Lord upon them and, thus, save untold numbers from the same fate.

Crimes against the innocent or great unrighteousness often result in the fall of entire nations. It wasn't necessarily poor politics which brought down Rome or other great civilizations throughout earth's long history. It was divine retribution in response to their wickedness and because they stoned the prophets and killed the Saints, often in the most cruel fashion. It wasn't because the inhabitants of Pompey innocently built their city too close to a volcano that brought about their destruction; it was because of unrighteousness. The volcano was simply the means of destruction. It wasn't poor leadership which brought the Nazi Party to its knees during World War II, but the wrath of God, who sent in the righteous to pound them into submission because of the atrocities they inflicted upon the house of Judah. It wasn't even the Lamanites who ultimately brought down the Nephites, but their own actions in turning away from the great light and knowledge God had given them and rejecting Jesus as their Savior (Morm. 6:17). In like manner, the Lord allowed the Spaniards to destroy many thousands of natives in South and Central America during the early days of colonization because of their perverted ways and their heinous practice of sacrificing untold numbers of innocent men, women, and children to their pagan gods. Did not millions die in these various instances, both of the righteous and

17

the wicked? Yes, and each are assigned an appropriate reward, with the righteous affixing the punishment for the wicked.

> And then shall it come to pass, that the spirits of those who are righteous are received into a state of happiness, which is called paradise, a state of rest, a state of peace, where they shall rest from all their troubles and from all care, and sorrow.
>
> Now this is the state of the souls of the wicked, yea, in darkness, and a state of awful, fearful looking for the fiery indignation of the wrath of God upon them; thus they remain in this state, as well as the righteous in paradise, until the time of their resurrection. (Alma 40:12, 14)

It is so difficult for us to see the big picture when our view of life extends over such a few short decades. We would do well to try and look beyond our narrow vision and gain a glimpse of the broader view of things—a view from God's perspective, for only he can truly see or discern what is best for his children in the long run. It may be years or even centuries before a nation or a people are ripe for destruction. Sadly, all too often the innocent suffer at the hands of the wicked before the destruction comes. But, they rest in peace.

> For the Lord suffereth the righteous to be slain that his justice and judgment may come upon the wicked; therefore ye need not suppose that the righteous are lost because they are slain; but behold, they do enter into the rest of the Lord their God. (Alma 60:13)

As sad as their deaths are, those who die in the Lord are spared any further indignities placed upon him by the wicked of the world.

> Wherefore, fear not even unto death; for in this world your joy is not full, but in me your joy is full. (D&C 101:36)

~ ~ ~

The decline of a nation or people is often so slow it is sometimes indiscernible to those who are living at the time. Satan presents his philosophies in such small, unrecognizable packages that they may seem innocent at first. He plays upon man's own lustful appetites and then caps it off by teaching him there is no God, thus there is no harm at all in enjoying the pleasures spread out before him. He also teaches a much diluted version of justice, which also has deadly consequences.

> And there shall also be many which shall say: Eat, drink, and be merry; nevertheless, fear God—he will justify in committing a little sin; yea, lie a little, take the advantage of one because of his words, dig a pit for thy neighbor; there is no harm in this; and do all these things, for tomorrow we die; and if it so be that we are guilty, God will beat us with a few stripes, and at last we shall be saved in the kingdom of God. (2 Ne. 28:8)

Anti-Christs, such as the one encountered by Alma in the Book of Mormon, teach that everyone will be saved regardless of their works or lack of them.

> And he also testified unto the people that all mankind should be saved at the last day, and that they need not fear nor tremble, but that they might lift up their heads and rejoice; for the Lord had created all men, and had also redeemed all men; and, in the end, all men should have eternal life. (Alma 1:4)

The Lord makes his position on that subject very clear.

> But behold, and fear, and tremble before God, for ye ought to tremble; for the Lord redeemeth none such that rebel against him and die in their sins; yea, even all those that have perished in their sins ever since the world began, that have wilfully rebelled against God, that have known the commandments of God, and would not keep them; these are they that have no part in the first resurrection.
>
> Therefore ought ye not to tremble? For salvation cometh to none such; for the Lord hath redeemed none such; yea, neither can the Lord redeem such; for he cannot deny himself; for he cannot deny justice when it has its claim. (Mosiah 15:26–27)

Unfortunately, the philosophies of men are being heralded from the housetops by numerous groups, some of which expand their philosophies to include mind control or self aggrandizement—thus diminishing man's need for God. Others teach even more insidious doctrines which embrace actual perversions such as found in the Occult. All too many of them are flourishing today—just as they did in days of old.

> For the time speedily shall come that all churches which are built up to get gain, and all those who are built up to get power over the flesh, and those who are built up to become popular in the eyes of the world, and those who seek the lusts of the flesh and the things of the world, and to do all manner of iniquity; yea, in fine, all those who belong to the kingdom of the devil are they who need fear, and tremble, and quake; they are those who must be brought low in the dust; they are those who must be consumed as stubble; and this is according to the words of the prophet. (1 Ne. 22:23)

We must safeguard ourselves and our families against such assault upon righteousness with all the strength that is in us lest we find our own salvation in peril on judgment day.

> Prepare your souls for that glorious day when justice shall be administered unto the righteous, even the day of judgment, that ye may not shrink with awful fear; that ye may not remember your awful guilt in perfectness, and be constrained to exclaim: Holy, holy are thy judgments, O Lord God Almighty—but I know my guilt; I transgressed thy law, and my transgressions are mine; and the devil hath obtained me, that I am a prey to his awful misery. (2 Ne. 9:46)

Because of the flesh and the weaknesses inherent in all mankind, the family of God must be stirred up to repentance from time to time, for left to themselves they might spiral out of control and be lost to Satan. Sometimes the only way to get their attention is to preach hell, fire, and damnation, just as was done in the days of Enos.

> And there was nothing save it was exceeding harsh-
> ness, preaching and prophesying of wars, and contentions,
> and destructions, and continually reminding them of death, and
> the duration of eternity, and the judgments and the power of
> God, and all these things—stirring them up continually to
> keep them in the fear of the Lord. (Enos 1:23)

So much temptation surrounds us that it is no wonder the Lord instructed our prayers to include the pleading words, "lead us not into temptation" (Luke 11:4), that we be not led astray by the devil, "for behold, he rewardeth you no good thing" (Alma 34:39). He admonishes us:

> Verily, verily, I say unto you, ye must watch and pray
> always, lest ye be tempted by the devil, and ye be led away
> captive by him. (3 Ne. 18:15)

~ ~ ~

While temptations of every imaginable kind have always plagued mankind, one of Satan's favorites is the worship of idols, for nothing leads men away from God faster. Those who foolishly choose to worship idols are allowed to make them in any image they like and can call upon them for anything their hearts desire, right or wrong.

> Yea, wo unto those that worship idols, for the devil of
> all devils delighteth in them. (2 Ne. 9:37)

Both biblical and historical records indicate entire civilizations have turned their backs on God in favor of idol worship over the long history of the world—idols of stone or mythical gods of one kind or another. They created gods for every season; gods to assure fertility or victory in battle, and even gods which sanction lustful behavior. It is no wonder God turns his face from those who embrace such evil practices, for such gods can offer his children nothing, only sin. Moreover he is a jealous God. After creating the world for them and every good thing possible, after fighting their battles and preserving them against their enemies time and time again, after providing the bounties of life and happiness and providing for their ultimate salvation, they turn to images of wood or gods of stone. Such practices incur his full wrath and often brings down the entire nation that embraces such perversion.

> Ye shall make you no idols nor graven image, neither rear you up a standing image, neither shall ye set up any image of stone in your land, to bow down unto it: for I am the LORD your God. (Lev. 26:1)

Not only did certain gentile and heathen nations worship idols throughout the centuries, but it was that very practice which brought about the dissolution of the entire nation of Israel. They began to build up high places for the worship of idols and burnt incense to them both day and night. Nothing could have displeased the Lord more and ultimately cost the Israelites dearly, for they provoked Jehovah to anger (2 Kgs. 17:11).

We, too, must be wary of worshiping false gods. Although not in the same category, the worship of wealth, power, or fame, can also have deadly consequences. Satan's trail of lies and plots for our souls knows no bounds and he will use any tactic he can to lead us away from the light. But, let him take notice, the gates of hell shall not prevail, for the wicked will soon be swept away.

> Wherefore, verily I say, let the wicked take heed, and let the rebellious fear and tremble; and let the unbelieving hold their lips, for the day of wrath shall come upon them as a whirlwind, and all flesh shall know that I am God. (D&C 63:6)

Our great Father and God has been there for his children from the very beginning of time, and will not forsake them now at this eleventh hour. Did he not instruct the Angel of Death to pass over the Children of Israel when the plague of death was pronounced upon the firstborn of Egypt? So must we trust that he will preserve us in these last days as well. Our job then is to watch and wait and prepare ourselves to meet the Savior when he comes to save the world.

> And angels shall fly through the midst of heaven, crying with a loud voice, sounding the trump of God, saying: Prepare ye, prepare ye, O inhabitants of the earth; for the judgment of our God is come. Behold, and lo, the Bridegroom cometh; go ye out to meet him. (D&C 88:92)

Prepare ye, prepare ye, we are warned. Yet how many of us neglect that admonition. Are we praying daily and searching the scriptures for the answers to life's problems? Have we prepared our families for every needful thing? Even our temporal needs are important in this day of uncertainly.

Brigham Young teaches us:

> Who are deserving of praise? The persons who take care of themselves or the ones who always trust in the great mercies of the Lord to take care of them? It is just as consistent to expect that the Lord will supply us with fruit when we do not plant the trees; or that when we do not plow and sow and are saved the labor of harvesting, we should cry to the Lord to save us from want, as to ask him to save us from the consequences of our own folly, disobedience and waste.[1]

It is always wise to be prepared against any unforeseen emergencies, but the counsel to be prepared to defend ourselves, our nation and even the Church and kingdom, if needed, is just as valid, for the forces of evil are at our very doors. That counsel is brought home loud and clear by Brigham Young in his instruction to the early Saints.

> We all believe that the Lord will fight our battles; but how? Will he do it while we are unconcerned and make no effort whatsoever for our own safety when an enemy is upon us? If we make no efforts to guard our towns, our houses, our cities, our wives and children, will the Lord guard them for us? He will not; but if we pursue the opposite course and strive to help him to accomplish his designs,

then will he fight our battles. We are baptized for the remission of sins; but it would be quite as reasonable to expect remission of sins without baptism, as to expect the Lord to fight our battles without our taking every precaution to be prepared to defend ourselves. The Lord requires us to be quite as willing to fight our own battles as to have him fight them for us. If we are not ready for an enemy when he comes upon us, we have not lived up to the requirements of him who guides the ship of Zion, or who dictates the affairs of his Kingdom.[2]

And what of our duties to strengthen ourselves and our families spiritually against the onslaught of the negative and hateful influences that surround us on all sides? Our children are especially vulnerable. It is no secret that Satan desires our little ones, for with them comes the world. The collapsing morals of our nation, along with the violence which fills our streets has deep roots in the breakdown of the family. Thus, one of our greatest responsibilities in this Saturday night of time is to strengthen our homes and families against the despicable tactics of the father of lies. Unfortunately, his evil influence has become so strong that great mists of darkness now encircle the globe and it is becoming more and more difficult to see the light.

And the mists of darkness are the temptations of the devil, which blindeth the eyes, and hardens the hearts of the children of men, and leadeth them away into broad roads, that they perish and are lost. (1 Ne. 12:17)

Thankfully, Satan's days are nearly over, and those who embrace his demonic wiles will soon have their just rewards.

Yea, they are grasped with death, and hell; and death, and hell, and the devil, and all that have been seized therewith must stand before the throne of God, and be judged according to their works, from whence they must go into the place prepared for them, even a lake of fire and brimstone, which is endless torment. (2 Ne. 28:23)

How tragic to be consigned to a lake of fire and brimstone which, according to the scriptures, is considered a second death, "for they are cut off as to things pertaining to righteousness" (Hel. 14:18).

> And now behold, I say unto you then cometh a death, even a second death, which is a spiritual death; then is a time that whosoever dieth in his sins, as to a temporal death, shall also die a spiritual death; yea, he shall die as to things pertaining unto righteousness. (Alma 12:16)

While Satan offers every delight in the world, the eternal ramifications of following him are so terrible and so far reaching that it is no wonder the Lord cries repentance so often and chastises his children when they sin or go astray. And, it is no wonder a sacrificial lamb was prepared from the very foundations of the world for our redemption. Can we ever doubt his love again? Can we ever take his constant appeals to repent lightly again, or ignore that advice, or even put it off another day?

> For behold, if ye have procrastinated the day of your repentance even until death, behold, ye have become subjected to the spirit of the devil, and he doth seal you his; therefore, the Spirit of the Lord hath withdrawn from you, and hath no place in you, and the devil hath all power over you; and this is the final state of the wicked. (Alma 34:35)

How terrible to be out of the reach of righteousness. Would not those who were truly aware of such a fate be willing to change their worldly ways and turn back again to the Lord?

> Wherefore, he saves all except them—they shall go away into everlasting punishment, which is endless punishment, which is eternal punishment, to reign with the devil and his angels in eternity, where their worm dieth not, and the fire is not quenched, which is their torment. (D&C 76:44)

While the righteous do not delight in the destruction of those who have gone astray, at some point, when every opportunity to repent has been met with rebuff, their fate is sealed and hell awaits them. But, those who overcome the evil influences of the Prince of Darkness and endure to the end will reap glorious rewards. Thus, as James says, "resist the devil, and he will flee from you" (James 4:7).

Without a doubt, the last days are upon us and we are already seeing the prophesied tribulations of the end of times. But with God by our sides and by putting on the full armor of righteousness, we will withstand the blows of the coming days and be worthy to dwell with the Lord and all those who abide the day for a millennium of peace.

> Put on the whole armour of God, that ye may be able to stand against the wiles of the devil. . . .
>
> Stand therefore, having your loins girt about with truth, and having on the breastplate of righteousness;
>
> And your feet shod with the preparation of the gospel of peace;
>
> Above all, taking the shield of faith, wherewith ye shall be able to quench all the fiery darts of the wicked.
>
> And take the helmet of salvation, and the sword of the Spirit, which is the word of God:
>
> Praying always with all prayer and supplication in the Spirit, and watching thereunto with all perseverance and supplication for all saints. (Eph. 6:11, 14–18)

The kingdom has been given to the saints until the storm is over. Thus, we must not fear, for God is at the helm and directing the work at hand.

> Fear not, little flock, the kingdom is yours until I come. Behold, I come quickly. Even so. Amen. (D&C 35:27)

~ ~ ~

Notes

1. Brigham Young, *Journal of Discourses,* 12:243–44.
2. Ibid., 11:131.

Chapter Three

The Gathering and Protection
of the Righteous

*And I will gather my people together as a man
gathereth his sheaves into the floor. (3 Ne. 20:18)*

Throughout the history of man, our Father and God has
nurtured his children with all the care of a loving parent and
watched attentively as generation after generation struggled
between the forces of good and evil. He rejoiced over the
righteous, but, because of the eternal nature of agency, could
only watch in silence as far too many succumbed to the enticings of the devil. He groaned under the weight of their wickedness, yet loved them enough to offer up his only Begotten Son
as a sacrificial Lamb in their behalf—that same son, even his
first-born, he who worked so valiantly to save his brothers and
sisters, yet was so often rejected by them.

O, ye nations of the earth, how often would I have
gathered you together as a hen gathereth her chickens under
her wings, but ye would not!

How oft have I called upon you by the mouth of my
servants, and by the ministering of angels, and by mine own
voice, and by the voice of thunderings, and by the voice of
tempests, and by the voice of earthquakes, and great hail-
storms, and by the voice of famines and pestilence of every
kind, and by the great sound of a trump, and by the voice of
judgment, and by the voice of mercy all the day long, and

by the voice of glory and honor and the riches of eternal life, and would have saved you with an everlasting salvation, but ye would not! (D&C 43:24-25)

In spite of God's long suffering and patience in their behalf, the day has finally come when the cup of his indignation is full to overflowing, and his terrible wrath will soon be felt by all those who have turned their backs on him. Before that terrible time comes, however, he must separate the wheat from the tares, that the righteous might be gathered together and protected before the sword of his justice falls upon the wicked.

> Therefore, I must gather together my people, according to the parable of the wheat and the tares, that the wheat may be secured in the garners to possess eternal life, when I shall come in the Kingdom of my Father to reward every man according as his work shall be. (D&C 101:65)

As the end times approach and our anxieties concerning our safety escalates, we can be comforted in the knowledge that the God has promised his righteous children protection from the earliest of times and will not suffer that they be destroyed along with the wicked. He often does so by gathering them out from among the unrepentant and into regions of safety before his anger is unleashed upon those who have given themselves over to Lucifer.

The Prophet Joseph Smith teaches us:

> In addition to all temporal blessings, there is no other way for the Saints to be saved in these last days (than by the gathering) as the concurrent testimony of all the holy prophets clearly proves, for it is written—"They shall come from the east, and be gathered from the west, the north shall give up, and the south shall keep not back. The sons of God shall be gathered from afar, and his daughters from the ends of the earth." It is also concurrent testimony of all the prophets, that this gathering together of all the Saints, must take place before the Lord comes to "take vengeance upon the ungodly," and "to be glorified and admired by all those who obey the gospel."[1]

We, as Latter-day Saints, are Saturday's warriors in every sense of the word and must, therefore, help in the work of gathering.

Therefore, tarry, and labor and labor diligently, that you may be perfected in your ministry to go forth among the gentiles for the last time, as many as the mouth of the Lord shall name, to bind up the law and seal up the testimony, and to prepare the saints for the hour of judgment which is to come;

That their souls may escape the wrath of God, the desolation of abomination which awaits the wicked. . . .

For not many days hence and the earth shall tremble and reel to and fro as a drunken man; and the sun shall hide his face, and refuse to give light; and the moon shall be bathed in blood; and the stars shall become exceedingly angry, and shall cast themselves down as a fig that falleth from off a fig tree.

And after your testimony cometh wrath and indignation upon the people. For after your testimony cometh the testimony of earthquakes, that shall cause groaning in the midst of her, and men shall fall upon the ground and shall not be able to stand.

And also cometh the testimony of the voice of thundering, and lightning, and the voice of tempests, and the voice of the waves of the sea heaving themselves beyond their bounds.

And all things shall be in commotion; and surely, men's hearts shall fail them; for fear shall come upon all people. (D&C 88:84-85, 87–91)

In studying the parable of the olive tree, we can see just how carefully the Lord of the vineyard has nurtured his garden over the last six millenniums. From the earliest of times he has placed his children in those various circumstances which would be for their ultimate good and well being, even when they understood it not. He planted and transplanted them in areas best suited to their individual needs, over and over again, constantly nourishing them by the voice of his prophets, by the scriptures, and by his Holy Spirit, yet all too often they murmured and rose up in rebellion against him.

In the beginning, the early patriarchs stood solid in the faith and taught their families to love God. Yet, right from those earliest days the devil had great hold over the hearts of the people. By the end of the first two thousand years of this earth's temporal existence, the world was so steeped in idolatry and sin that it was ripe for destruction. Tragically, not only had they sealed their own fate, but their posterity's as well. The only way to save the myriads of Father's children yet unborn would be to sweep the wicked away and begin again. Thus, the Lord began the slow and systematic process of weeding his garden so the few remaining vines would not be choked out by those weeds and briars that had taken over the vineyard.

In his efforts to save the righteous the Prophet Noah began a lengthy mission to gather out any and all who would listen. The cry of repentance was heard upon every hill and in every valley as Noah, under the direction of the Lord himself, began the task of weeding the vineyard and saving what little fruit was still on the vine. One from a family and two from a city responded until all the righteous were gathered out and directed to the city of Enoch where they became a Zion people. Then, when his mission was completed, the Lord physically carried the people of Enoch up and away from the earth before opening the windows of heaven and unleashing the rains upon the ungodly (Gen. 7:11). The deluge continued for forty days and forty nights, and the waters increased upon the earth until every valley was filled and every mountain covered, and those who stoned the prophets and turned their backs on God were utterly and completely destroyed from off the face of the earth.

That catastrophic episode in history is our most dramatic example of God's dealings with his children in regard to the separating of the wheat from the tares and the gathering and protecting of the righteous before destroying the wicked. How can we read the beautiful story of Enoch and his people, and marvel at the workings of God in their behalf, and still doubt that God will protect those of us in these latter days from the calamities which lie ahead? Rest assured that he will. Just as he directed the righteous during Noah's day to the city of Enoch, so also will he direct those in our day to the stakes of Zion for protection—and also to a city much like that of Enoch's day which is destined to be built just prior to the Savior's Second Advent.

> And it shall be called the New Jerusalem, a land of peace, a city of refuge, a place of safety for the saints of the Most High God;
>
> And the glory of the Lord shall be there, and the terror of the Lord also shall be there, insomuch that the wicked will not come unto it, and it shall be called Zion. (D&C 45:66–67)

The tribulation of the last days will eventually escalate to the point where there will be no peace except in Zion and her satellite cities and stakes.

> Verily I say unto you all: arise and shine forth, that thy light may be for a standard for the nations:
>
> And that the gathering together upon the land of Zion, and upon her stakes, may be for a defense, and for a refuge from the storm, and from the wrath when it shall be poured out without mixture upon the whole earth. (D&C 115:5–6)

Not only will the righteous find sanctuary in Zion, but the time will come when they will be the only people on earth who will be at peace.

> And it shall come to pass among the wicked, that every man that will not take his sword against his neighbor must needs flee unto Zion for safety.
>
> And there shall be gathered unto it out of every nation under heaven; and it shall be the only people that shall not be at war one with another.

> And it shall be said among the wicked: Let us not go up to battle against Zion, for the inhabitants of Zion are terrible; wherefore we cannot stand.
>
> And it shall come to pass that the righteous shall be gathered out from among all nations, and shall come to Zion, singing with songs of everlasting joy. (D&C 45:68–71)

As the cry of repentance goes forth throughout the world, those who respond will be gathered into the fold of Christ and into the safety of Zion where they shall be protected against the terrible storms destined to lay waste the wicked nations of the world.

> Wherefore the decree hath gone forth from the Father that they shall be gathered in unto one place upon the face of the land, to prepare their hearts and be prepared in all things against the day when tribulation and desolation are sent forth upon the wicked.
>
> For the hour is nigh and the day soon at hand when the earth is ripe; and all the proud and they that do wickedly shall be as stubble; and I will burn them up, saith the Lord of Hosts, that wickedness shall not be upon the earth;
>
> For the hour is nigh, and that which was spoken by mine apostles must be fulfilled; for as they spoke so shall it come to pass;
>
> For I will reveal myself from heaven with power and great glory, with all the hosts thereof, and dwell in righteousness with men on earth a thousand years, and the wicked shall not stand. (D&C 29:8–11)

The scriptures are clear on this matter—the vengeance of the Lord will not fall upon the wicked nations of the world until after the righteous have all been gathered out from among them and into safe havens.

We might remember how the cities of Sodom and Gomorrah were destroyed only after Lot and his family departed. In like fashion, Jerusalem was not destroyed until Lehi and his family were out of harm's way. When the plagues fell upon the

Egyptians, the children of Israel were spared, and when they crossed the Red Sea, the waters did not fold in upon themselves until the children of Israel were safely through the sea and on the other shore.

Similar instances can be found in the Book of Mormon. In third Nephi we read of the terrible destruction which laid waste numerous wicked cities at the time of the Savior's death. But only after their inhabitants had cast the righteous out from among them.

> And behold, the city of Laman, and the city of Josh, and the city of Gad, and the city of Kishkumen, have I caused to be burned with fire, and the inhabitants thereof, because of their wickedness in casting out the prophets, and stoning those whom I did send to declare unto them concerning their wickedness and abominations.
>
> And because they did cast them all out, *that there were none righteous among them,* I did send down fire and destroy them, that their wickedness and abominations might be hid from before my face, that the blood of the prophets and the saints whom I sent among them might not cry unto me from the ground against them. (3 Ne. 9:10–11; emphasis added)

While such instances reveal that the Lord's patience will only extend so long, they also reveal that the honest in heart need not fear, for throughout the long history of the world, the Lord has always removed the righteous from targeted areas before his mighty sword of justice falls upon the unrepentant.

Now, such promised protection does not exempt the Saints from tribulation, especially those instigated by the great and abominable church which is destined to rise to power sometime in the future. But, the scriptures are quick to emphasize that all they who fight against Zion shall eventually be destroyed.

> And every nation which shall war against thee, O house of Israel, shall be turned one against another, and they shall fall into the pit which they digged to ensnare the people of the Lord. And all that fight against Zion shall be destroyed,

33

and that great whore, who hath perverted the right ways of the Lord, yea, that great and abominable church, shall tumble to the dust and great shall be the fall of it. (1 Ne. 22:14)

As has been the nature of things from the very beginning, the blessings of protection are conditional upon man's righteousness. Thus, if any in Zion fall victim to sin, they too must repent to be worthy of such divine care.

Therefore, verily, thus saith the Lord, let Zion rejoice, for this is Zion—THE PURE IN HEART; therefore, let Zion rejoice, while all the wicked shall mourn.

For behold, and lo, vengeance cometh speedily upon the ungodly as the whirlwind; and who shall escape it?

The Lord's scourge shall pass over by night and by day, and the report thereof shall vex all people; yea, it shall not be stayed until the Lord come;

For the indignation of the Lord is kindled against their abominations and all their wicked works.

Nevertheless, Zion shall escape if she observe to do all things whatsoever I have commanded her.

But if she observe not to do whatsoever I have commanded her, I will visit her according to all her works, with sore affliction, with pestilence, with plague, with sword, with vengeance, with devouring fire.

Nevertheless, let it be read this once to her ears, that I, the Lord, have accepted of her offering; and if she sin no more none of these things shall come upon her;

And I will bless her with blessings, and multiply a multiplicity of blessings upon her, and upon her generations forever and ever, saith the Lord your God. Amen. (D&C 97:21–28)

The Lord also makes it clear that those who fight *not* against Zion shall likewise be preserved.

And blessed are the Gentiles, they of whom the prophet has written; for behold, if it so be that they shall repent and

fight not against Zion, and do not unite themselves to that
great and abominable church, they shall be saved. (2 Ne. 6:12)

Now, if some who vex the Saints during the final sifting
process are not yet ripe for immediate destruction, the Lord
will simply lead those in peril to safer territory, such as those
in the early days of the restoration who were in mortal danger
from evil men who were determined to destroy them. At their
darkest hour, the Lord wrapped his mighty cloak about the
Saints and preserved them from extermination by allowing
them to be driven from their homes and into a distant land destined to be a refuge for them and a safe harbor for their posterity. The elements at that hour were severe and the hearts of
many were faint as they began their long trek west, but with
his out-stretched hand the Lord led them across the country to
the Salt Lake Valley where he could bless them and where they
could grow in strength and become a mighty people. High in
the tops of the Rocky Mountains the Lord watched over his
little flock. Their lot was not an easy one and trials of every
nature rose up before them, but God held them in the palm of
his hand until they tamed the land and flourished as a people.
Thus, we can see that the Lord will use any means he can to
preserve his people in their times of need.

~ ~ ~

While many of the prophecies concerning the last days
are yet to happen, many have already been fulfilled. The everlasting gospel has been restored along with the keys from all
past dispensations of time. The golden plates have been trans-
lated by the gift and power of God and have gone forth
throughout the world to testify of his Lordship, and the gathering of the righteous from the four corners of the world
has begun. Even so, much concerning the destruction of the
world is still before us, and much concerning the gathering of
Israel is yet in the future.

While the gathering of the Jews to their homeland has already commenced, the time will come when many more will return to the land of their fathers.

> And I will remember the covenant which I have made with my people; and I have covenanted with them that I would gather them together in mine own due time, that I would give unto them again the land of their fathers for their inheritance, which is the land of Jerusalem, which is the promised land unto them forever, saith the Father. (3 Ne. 20:29)

Great tribulation will continue in that land however, until the Lord himself comes to save his people from those who have gone up against the children of Judah.

~ ~ ~

There will come a time when the mission to the gentile nations is completed. At that time the mission to the House of Israel will begin in earnest, and thousands upon thousands from Israel will be gathered to the lands of their inheritance, including the ten lost tribes.

> At that day shall the work of the Father commence among all the dispersed of my people, yea, even the tribes which have been lost, which the Father hath led away out of Jerusalem.
>
> Yea, the work shall commence among all the dispersed of my people, with the Father to prepare the way whereby they may come unto me, that they may call on the Father in my name.
>
> Yea, and then shall the work commence, with the Father among all nations in preparing the way whereby his people may be gathered home to the land of their inheritance.
>
> And they shall go out from all nations; and they shall not go out in haste, nor go by flight, for I will go before them, saith the Father, and I will be their rearward. (3 Ne. 21:26–29)

In connection with the gathering of Israel, the Lamanites, who also enjoy that lineage, will come to know God and will join with the Saints in building up the New Jerusalem in preparation for the Lord's triumphant return. Speaking of that remnant of Jacob, the Lord said:

> And behold, this people will I establish in this land, unto the fulfilling of the covenant which I made with your father Jacob; and it shall be a New Jerusalem. And the powers of heaven shall be in the midst of this people; yea, even I will be in the midst of you. (3 Ne. 20:22)

When tribe after tribe pass through the gates of Zion, the hills will sing their everlasting praises to God and the lost sons of Israel will mingle with the gathered of Ephraim and together they will wait upon the triumphant return of Jehovah.

The Prophet Joseph Smith teaches us of that glorious time when the Saints will be gathered together.

> It shall no longer be said, the Lord lives that brought up the children of Israel out of the land of Egypt, but the Lord lives that brought up the children of Israel from the land of the north, and from all the lands whither He has driven them. That day is one, all important to all men.
>
> In speaking of the gathering, we mean to be understood as speaking of it according to scripture, the gathering of the elect of the Lord out of every nation on earth, and bringing them to the place of the Lord of Hosts, when the city of righteousness shall be built, and where the people shall be one heart and one mind, when the Savior comes; yea where the people shall walk with God like Enoch and be free from sin. The word of the Lord is precious; and when we read that the veil spread over all nations will be destroyed, and the pure in heart see God, and reign with Him a thousand years on earth, we want all honest men to have a chance to gather and build up a city of righteousness, where even upon the bells of the horses shall be written "Holiness to the Lord."[2]

In a discourse given by the prophet Joseph Smith, regarding the assembling of saints to Zion, we read:

The building up of Zion is a cause that has interested
the people of God in every age; it is a theme upon which
prophets, priests and kings have dwelt with peculiar delight;
they have looked forward with joyful anticipation to the day
in which we live; and fired with heavenly and joyful antic-
ipations they have sung and written and prophesied of this
our day; but they died without the sight; we are the favored
people that God had made choice of to bring about the Latter-day glory; it is left for us to see, participate in and help
to roll forward the Latter-day glory, "The dispensation of
the fullness of times, when God will gather together all
things that are in heaven and that are upon the earth, even
in one," when the Saints of God will be gathered in one
from every nation, and kindred, and people, and tongue,
when the Jews will be gathered together into one, the
wicked will also be gathered together to be destroyed, as
spoken of by the prophets; the Spirit of God will also dwell
with his people, and be withdrawn from the rest of the
nations, and all things whether in heaven or on earth will be
in one, even in Christ. The heavenly Priesthood will unite
with the earthly, to bring about those great purposes; and
whilst we are thus united in one common cause, to roll forth
the kingdom of God, the heavenly Priesthood are not idle
spectators, the Spirit of God will be showered down from
above, and it will dwell in our midst. The blessings of the
Most High will rest upon our tabernacles, and our name will
be handed down to future ages; our children will rise up
and call us blessed; and generations yet unborn will dwell
with peculiar delight upon the scenes that we have passed
through, the privations that we have endured; the untiring
zeal that we have manifested; the all but insurmountable
difficulties that we have overcome in laying the foundation
of a work that brought about the glory and blessing which
they will realize; a work that God and angels have contem-
plated with delight for generations past; that fired the souls
of the ancient patriarchs and prophets; a work that is destined to bring about the destruction of the powers of darkness, the renovation of the earth, the glory of God, and the
salvation of the human family.[3]

~ ~ ~

Although the Saints have been promised protection from the major calamities of the last days, as the end times approach we cannot say that there will not be pain or death for any of the Saints before the winding up scene is over. Some may well succumb to the weakness of the flesh or to the woes brought about by those whose mission it is to destroy and lay waste. Yet, those who fall will have a glorious reward—equal to that of all the other martyrs who have given their lives in the cause of righteousness, and will help to assure the wicked receive their just rewards. But, the Saints as a whole will prevail over their enemies from this very moment onward, and when the time is right will be gathered out from those areas destined for destruction and given sanctuary within the stakes of Zion (see D&C 103:5–7).

We must understand, however, that to be afforded the protection of the Almighty, we must live lives worthy of his divine care. We must repent and forsake evil and call upon Father daily, for God will not forsake those who bend the knee and humble themselves before him. He will wrap those who love him in his mighty arms and carry them upon his shoulders, if needed, to preserve them from the destruction that must ultimately come upon the wicked. Therefore, we must not for a moment let our eyes stray from the path of righteousness nor let loose our grasp from the iron rod, for Satan and his hosts stand close and wish to tear us from our safe moorings. If we are not planted firmly in our testimonies and doing all that we can to live in accordance with the light and knowledge God has given us, he will surely find the way to tempt us into forbidden paths. The gathering has begun, and soon the honorable and righteous will find peace in the glory of a new terrestrial world.

Harold B. Lee gives us these insightful words as to where the Saints should gather and where to look for direction.

The spirit of gathering has been with the church from the days of the restoration. Those who are of the blood of Israel have a righteous desire after they are baptized, to gather together with the body of the Saints at the designated place. . . . After designating certain places in that day where the saints were to gather the Lord said this:

"Until the day cometh, when there is found no more room for them; and then I have other places which I will appoint unto them" (D&C 101:21).[4]

Thus the Lord has clearly placed the responsibility for directing the work of gathering in the hands of the leaders of the Church to whom he will reveal his will where and when such gathering would take place in the future.

It would be well, before the frightening events concerning the fulfillment of all God's promises and predictions are upon us, that the Saints in every land prepare themselves and look forward to the instruction that shall come to them from the First Presidency of this Church as to where they shall be gathered and not be disturbed in their feelings until such instruction is given to them as it is revealed by the Lord to the proper authority.[5]

Elder Bruce R. McConkie instructs us:

We do not know when the calamities and troubles of the last days will fall upon any of us as individuals or upon bodies of the Saints. The Lord deliberately withholds from us the day and hour of his coming and of the tribulations which shall proceed it—all as part of the testing and probationary experiences of mortality. He simply tells us to watch and be ready.

We can rest assured that if we have done all in our power to prepare for whatever lies ahead, he will help us with whatever else we need.

He rained manna from heaven upon all Israel, six days each week for forty years, lest they perish for want of bread. . . . (See Ex. 16:3–4, 35.)

During forty years in the wilderness the clothes worn

by all Israel waxed not old and their shoes wore not out . . . (See Deut. 29:5.)

When there was a famine in the land, at Elijah's word, a certain barrel of meal did not waste, and a certain cruse of oil did not fail, until the Lord sent again rain on the earth. And it is worthy of note, as Jesus said, that though there were many widows in Israel, unto only one was Elijah sent. (See 1 Kgs. 17:10–16.)

We do not say that all of the Saints will be spared and saved from the coming day of desolation. But we do say there is no promise of safety and no promise of security except for those who love the Lord and who seek to do all the commands.[6]

Elder Harold B. Lee instructs us that it is not so much *where* we live but *how* to live.

I know now that the place of safety in this world is not in any given place; it doesn't make so much difference where we live; but the all-important thing is how we live, and have found that . . . security can come to Israel only when they keep the commandments, when they live so that they can enjoy the companionship, the direction, the comfort, and the guidance of the Holy Spirit of the Lord, when they are willing to listen to these men whom God has set here to preside as His mouthpieces, and when we obey the counsels of the Church.[7]

Our strength, then, does not lie in our physical surroundings as much as it depends on our worthiness before the Lord, Thus, strengthening ourselves and our families spiritually should be our highest priority.

~ ~ ~

Notes

1. Smith, *History of the Church,* 4:272.
2. Ibid., 2:357.
3. Ibid., 4:608–10.

4. Lee, *Improvement Era* (June 1948): 320.
5. Ibid.
6. McConkie, "Stand Independent," 93.
7. Lee, CR, (April 1943) 129.

Chapter Four

The Destruction of the Wicked

To lift up your voice as with the sound of a trump,
both long and loud, and cry repentance unto a crooked
and perverse generation, preparing the way of the
Lord for his second coming. (D&C 34:6)

That same veil of darkness which covered the earth in
Noah's day has been settling over the earth in our day as well,
and an unprecedented spiritual decay is eroding our world.
The cleverly disguised philosophies of the Prince of Darkness
are influencing our minds and thinking more than at any other
time in history. And because the time is short, every diabolic
scheme he can conjure up is now being employed to corrupt
the hearts of men and lead them down to hell. Thus, that great
battle, which began in heaven, continues still upon the earth as
Lucifer and his demonic soldiers fight for the very souls of men.

Unfortunately, the war between good and evil is escalating at a dizzying pace, and far too many of God's children
have already succumbed to the lure of wealth, fame, power or
mortal appetites. They have ears that hear not, and eyes that
turn from the light. They have become hard in their hearts and
past feeling and deny the power of Christ while boasting of
their own cunning and strength. The time will shortly come,
however, when those who love darkness more than light will
feel the power of the Lord, God Almighty as they never have
before and will soon reap the rewards of the damned.

~ ~ ~

Although tribulation is at our very doors, our course should be set solidly in the faith in these last days, for the devil and his angels are lurking, not just in the shadows, but in broad daylight, and using every scheme at their command to lure us into forbidden paths. Therefore, we must follow the council of the Brethren closely and be ever watchful lest we, too, fall victim to Lucifer's enticings.

In *The Teachings of the Prophet Joseph Smith,* we are taught in whom to place our trust:

> As a church and a people it behooves us to be wise, to seek to know the will of God, and then be willing to do it; for, "Blessed is he that heareth the word of the Lord, and keepeth it," say the scriptures. "Watch and pray always," says our Savior, "That ye may be accounted worthy to escape the things that are to come on the earth, and to stand before the Son of Man." If Enoch, Abraham, Moses, and the Children of Israel, and all God's people were saved by keeping the commandments of God, we, if saved at all, shall be saved upon the same principle. As God governed Abraham, Isaac and Jacob as families, and the children of Israel as a nation; so we, as a church, must be under His guidance if we are to be prospered, preserved, and sustained. Our only confidence can be in God; our only wisdom obtained from Him; and He alone must be our protector and safeguard, spiritually and temporally, or we fall.[1]

The scriptures are filled with prophecies which teach us what to watch for and how to behave in these latter days. To the righteous they say watch, wait, and be ready. To the unrighteous they say repent, forsake your evil ways, come into the fold and be partakers of eternal life. Joseph Smith broadens our understanding of the importance of scripture study in preparing our minds for things to come when he admonishes us to:

> Search the revelations of God; study the prophecies, and rejoice that God grants unto the world Seers and Prophets. They are they who saw the mysteries of godliness; they saw

the flood before it came; they saw angels ascending and descending upon a ladder that reached from earth to heaven; they saw the stone cut out of the mountain, which filled the whole earth; they saw the Son of God come from the regions of bliss and dwell with men on earth; they saw the deliverer come out of Zion, and turn away ungodliness from Jacob; they saw the glory of the Lord when he showed the transfiguration of the earth on the Mount; they saw every mountain laid low and every valley exalted when the Lord was taking vengeance upon the wicked; they saw truth spring out of the earth, and righteousness look down from heaven in the last days, before the Lord came the second time to gather His elect; they saw the end of wickedness on earth, and the Sabbath of Creation crowned with peace; they saw the end of the glorious thousand years, when Satan was loosed for a little season; they saw the day of judgment when all men received according to their works, and they saw the heaven and the earth flee away to make room for the city of God, when the righteous receive an inheritance in Eternity. And, fellow sojourners upon earth, it is your privilege to purify yourselves and come up to the same glory, and see for yourselves, and know for yourselves. Ask, and it shall be given you; seek and ye shall find; knock, and it shall be opened unto you.[2]

The scriptures repeat over and over again the message that God will pour out his Spirit upon those who love him and that he will lead them as a hen leads her chicks to places of refuge within the stakes of Zion during times of peril.

In our modern scriptures the Lord reminds us of his concern for his Saints and gives these comforting words.

... I have decreed a decree which my people shall realize, inasmuch as they hearken from this very hour unto the counsel which I, the Lord their God, shall give unto them. Behold they shall, for I have decreed it, begin to prevail against mine enemies from this very hour. And by hearkening to observe all the words which I, the Lord their God, shall speak unto them, they shall never cease to prevail until the kingdoms of the world are subdued under my feet, and the earth is given unto the saints, to possess it forever and ever. (D&C 103:5–7)

Such a message should ease our minds and give us strength, for as much as we might wish it were otherwise, the work of the last days will commence whether we are ready or not. We cannot stop it with our lack of means or because of our insecurities or fears. We cannot pray for deliverance from the trials yet to come, for come they will. Thus, we must be prepared to fight the evil which surrounds us with God at our side and with the assurance that God is directing the work at hand.

In a comforting message to the Saints, President John Taylor reminds us of God's care and concern for the faithful.

> Before the Lord destroyed the old world, he directed Noah to prepare an ark; before the cities of Sodom and Gomorrah were destroyed, he told Lot to "flee to the mountains." Before Jerusalem was destroyed, Jesus gave his disciples warning, and told them to "flee out of it"; and before the destruction of the world a message is sent; after this, the nations will be judged, for God is now preparing His own Kingdom for His own reign; and will not be thwarted by any conflicting influence, or opposing power. The testimony of God is first to be made known, the standard is to be raised, the Gospel of the Kingdom is to be preached to all nations, the world is to be warned, and then comes the troubles. The whole world is in confusion; morally, politically, and religiously; but a voice was to be heard, "Come out of her, my people, that you partake not of her sins, and that ye receive not of her plagues."[3]

Unfortunately, as the inevitable destructions begin to fall, the wicked will continue to be deaf to the sermons of the Lord. They will continue to contend with their brothers to battle for land and possessions, and to satisfy their lust for power and blood. Moreover, it will be this very condition of pride and anger that will cause many of the ungodly to destroy themselves. That great serpent, the devil, will continue to have such hold over their hearts that there will be warring continually. Thus, cities and nations will fall by the sword and thousands upon thousands will be returned to the world of spirits. Most will go to their graves blaspheming God, but hopefully some will be brought to their knees in repentance.

> For the kingdom of the devil must shake, and they which belong to it must needs be stirred up unto repentance, or the devil will grasp them with his everlasting chains and they be stirred up to anger, and perish. (2 Ne. 28:19)

How many will repent when the world begins to feel the mighty power of the Lord remains to be seen, for already men's hearts are turning cold and unfeeling. Thus, the time for patience is quickly passing, and soon the world will experience the fiery wrath of the mighty Jehovah as they never have before.

Tempests, earthquakes, and natural disasters of every kind will continue to fall upon this generation and will increase in intensity in direct proportion to the rise of wickedness among us. But those awesome powers of *total* destruction will be reserved for the beginning of the seventh thousand period of time (see D&C 77:12). Only when every jot and tittle of prophecy has been fulfilled will the Lord begin the final work of cleansing the vineyard. When that fateful time comes, plague after plague will descend upon the earth and will reach such monumental proportions that great pockets of mankind will literally be wiped away.

Throughout the history of mankind the Lord has often allowed the wicked to destroy themselves through warring and contentions. But when the time is right, the great Jehovah will show forth his own mighty strength to the nations of the world and will command the elements themselves to combine against the unrepentant and to sweep them all away. When that terrible time comes, both heaven and earth will obey and all things will be in commotion. Stars will be hurled from their thrones and volcanos will spew their fiery venom into the sky. Wars and bloodshed will cause hearts to mourn, and the aftermath of worldwide conflict will leave great vapors of smoke and devastation of global proportions.

Numerous prophecies concerning the terrible destruction that await the wicked are yet to be fulfilled. Many of the prophesied plagues will rival those which fell upon Egypt just prior to the exodus of Moses and the children of Israel from bondage. But many will be far more serious. The world has not seen the likes of the terrible destructive forces that the Lord, God Almighty will ultimately unleash upon the wicked before he descends to rule the world. We read of just a few in the D&C:

> But, behold, I say unto you that before this great day shall come the sun shall be darkened, and the moon shall be turned into blood, and the stars shall fall from heaven, and there shall be greater signs in heaven above and in the earth beneath;
>
> And there shall be weeping and wailing among the hosts of men;
>
> And there shall be a great hailstorm sent forth to destroy the crops of the earth.
>
> And it shall come to pass, because of the wickedness of the world, that I will take vengeance upon the wicked, for they will not repent; for the cup of mine indignation is full; for behold, my blood shall not cleanse them if they hear me not. (D&C 29:14–17)

The various scriptures are filled with prophecies concerning the last days, far too many to dwell upon as we journey into a happier time. But just a few of those recorded by John reveal the magnitude of the destructive forces that will be poured out upon the wicked at the end of the world.

> The first angel sounded, and there followed hail and fire mingled with blood, and they were cast upon the earth: and the third part of trees was burnt up, and all green grass was burnt up.
>
> And the second angel sounded, and as it were a great

mountain burning with fire was cast into the sea: and the third part of the sea became blood;

And the third part of the creatures which were in the sea, and had life, died; and the third part of the ships were destroyed.

And the third angel sounded, and there fell a great star from heaven, burning as it were a lamp, and it fell upon the third part of the rivers, and upon the fountains of waters;

And the name of the star is called Wormwood: and the third part of the waters became wormwood; and many men died of the waters, because they were made bitter.

And the fourth angel sounded, and the third part of the sun was smitten, and the third part of the moon, and the third part of the stars; so as the third part of them was darkened, and the day shone not for a third part of it, and the night likewise.

And I beheld, and heard an angel flying through the midst of heaven, saying with a loud voice, Woe, woe, woe, to the inhabiters of the earth by reason of the other voices of the trumpet of the three angels, which are yet to sound! (Rev. 8:7–13)

A mighty cry will go up among the wicked as the plagues begin to fall, and they will curse God and blaspheme his name. Yet even in the face of such mighty works, most will not repent. Thus, their fate is sealed.

~ ~ ~

Now, in the midst of all this destruction the Lord will also be about the business of preparing the Saints for his ultimate return. He will make an appearance in the temple in the New Jerusalem, giving instruction and encouragement and setting in order the affairs of his kingdom. He will appear at the council at Adam-Ondi-Ahman where Father Adam will return the keys from all dispensations of time to the Savior in preparation for his rightful reign as Lord of Lords, and King of Kings over the whole earth (D&C 116:1). The Lord will appear to the Jews as well, during a time when they are struggling for survival against the greatest army ever assembled. The long anticipated battle of Armageddon will be so terrible that only the Lord Jesus and his heavenly army will be able to keep the children of Judah from being totally destroyed by the mighty forces destined to go up against them to battle. The voice of Jehovah will be heard throughout the heavens as he and his royal army swoop down upon the wicked.

> And I saw heaven opened, and behold a white horse; and he that sat upon him was called Faithful and True, and in righteousness he doth judge and make war.
>
> His eyes were as a flame of fire, and on his head were many crowns; and he had a name written, that no man knew, but he himself.
>
> And he was clothed with a vesture dipped in blood: and his name is called The Word of God.
>
> And the armies which were in heaven followed him upon white horses, clothed in fine linen, white and clean.
>
> And out of his mouth goeth a sharp sword, that with it he should smite the nations: and he shall rule them with a rod of iron: and he treadeth the winepress of the fierceness and wrath of Almighty God.
>
> And he hath on his vesture and on his thigh a name written, KING OF KINGS, AND LORD OF LORDS. (Rev. 19:11–16)

So many will lie dead on the battlefield after the Lord takes vengeance upon those who go up against Judah that the fowls of the earth will be called into the area to devour the corpses.

> And I saw an angel standing in the sun; and he cried with a loud voice, saying to all the fowls that fly in the midst of heaven, come and gather yourselves together unto the supper of the great God;
>
> That ye may eat the flesh of kings, and the flesh of captains, and the flesh of mighty men, and the flesh of horses, and of them that sit on them, and the flesh of all men, both free and bond, both small and great.
>
> And I saw the beast, and the kings of the earth, and

their armies, gathered together to make war against him that sat on the horse, and against his army.

And the beast was taken, and with him the false prophet that wrought miracles before him, with which he deceived them that had received the mark of the beast, and them that worshipped his image. These both were cast alive into a lake of fire burning with brimstone. (Rev. 19:17–20)

As marvelous as his appearance to the Jews will be, his final appearance will be even more glorious when he appears to all the world and declares himself king over the whole earth and everything in it. When that fateful day arrives, trumps will echo through the halls of the eternal mansions, and Christ with all his holy angels will descend upon the earth to burn the remainder of the wicked and to usher in his long anticipated millennial reign. The atmospheric clouds will bow before him as he rushes past, and the stars will flee as he descends upon the earth to reclaim the kingdoms of the world. This time, however, the entire world will witness that awesome occasion.

Behold, he cometh with clouds; and every eye shall see him, and they also which pierced him: and all kindreds of the earth shall wail because of him. Even so, Amen. (Rev. 1:7)

For those who stand in holy places the Second Coming will be a magnificent advent, but for the wicked, their time is past.

For the hour is nigh and the day soon at hand when the earth is ripe; and all the proud and they that do wickedly shall be as stubble; and I will burn them up, saith the Lord of Hosts, that wickedness shall not be upon the earth. (D&C 29:9)

The Second Coming will be of such grandeur that description fails as one tries to convey the wonder of those events destined to transpire at his appearance. President Charles W. Penrose has captured it beautifully in his article, "The Second Advent":

The tongue of man falters, and the pen drops from the hand of the writer, as the mind is rapt in contemplation of the sublime and awful majesty of His coming to take vengeance on the ungodly and to reign as King of the whole earth.

He comes! The earth shakes, and the tall mountains tremble, the mighty deep rolls back to the north in fear, and the rent skies glow like molten brass. He comes! The dead saints burst forth from their tombs, and "those who are alive and remain are caught up" with them to meet him. The ungodly rush to hide themselves from His presence and call upon the quivering rocks to cover them.

He comes! with all the host of the righteous glorified. The breath of His lips strikes death to the wicked. His glory is as a consuming fire. The proud and rebellious are as stubble; they are burned and left neither root nor branch. "He sweeps the earth as with the bosom of destruction." He deluges the earth with the fiery floods of His wrath, and the filthiness and abominations of the world are consumed. Satan and his dark hosts are taken and bound and the prince of the power of the air has lost his dominion, for He whose right it is to reign has come, and the kingdoms of this world have become the kingdoms of our Lord and of his Christ.[4]

Although great and wondrous changes have taken place in the earth since her creation, even greater changes will take place when the Savior makes his triumphant return. The upheavals will be so great at that time that even the hills will melt at his presence.

The mountains quake at him, and the hills melt, and the earth is burned at his presence, yea, the world, and all that dwell therein.

Who can stand before his indignation? Who can abide in the fierceness of his anger? His fury is poured out like fire, and the rocks are thrown down by him. (Nahum 1:5–6)

In Malachi we learn of those who are destined to be burned:

And I will come near to you to judgment; and I will be a swift witness against the sorcerers, and against the adulterers, and against false swearers, and against those that oppress the hireling in his wages, the widow, and the father-

less, and that turn aside the stranger from his right, and fear
not me, saith the LORD of hosts. (Mal. 3:5)

This grand climax will end the earth's telestial existence
with all its wars, bloodshed and irreverence for the things of
God. It will go out in a blaze of glory beyond any descriptions
our minds can employ and will mark the beginning of a new
age of peace and tranquility. And Lucifer, he who worked so
hard to corrupt mankind and thus glorify himself in his own
dominion, will be shackled at last.

> And he laid hold on the dragon, that old serpent, which
> is the Devil, and Satan, and bound him a thousand years,
>
> And cast him into the bottomless pit, and shut him up,
> and set a seal upon him, that he should deceive the nations
> no more, till the thousand years should be fulfilled: and
> after that he must be loosed a little season. (Rev. 20:2–3)

The City of Enoch, which was taken up before the flood
of Noah's day, will descend at the time of the Savior's coming.
That great city will be joined by the latter-day Zion, which will
ascend as did Enoch's city so long ago. This union will con-
stitute the marriage of the Lamb, Christ being the lamb and the
Church the bride.

> The Lord hath redeemed his people; And Satan is
> bound and time is no longer. The Lord hath gathered all
> things in one. The Lord hath brought down Zion from
> above. The Lord hath brought up Zion from beneath. (D&C
> 84:100)

With the advent of the Savior's triumphant return, comes
also the resurrection of the Just. These are they who are
members of the Church of the First Born—those who merit a
Celestial reward. Christ will come with an innumerable host of
glorified, resurrected beings who were resurrected in the
meridian of time when the Savior broke the bonds of death and
became the first fruits of the resurrection.

> And they who have slept in their graves shall come
> forth, for their graves shall be opened; and they also shall be
> caught up to meet him in the midst of the pillar of heaven.
> (D&C 88:97)

Words cannot express the magnificence of that occasion
when grave after grave will be opened and a myriad of glorified beings will rise from their entombment and be carried up
to greet the Savior in the clouds of heaven. Through all the
eons of time we have waited for this day—a day of triumph
over the wages of sin and corruption.

> For the Lord himself shall descend from heaven with
> a shout, with the voice of the archangel, and with the trump
> of God: and the dead in Christ shall rise first:
>
> Then we which are alive and remain shall be caught
> up together with them in the clouds, to meet the Lord in the
> air: and so shall we ever be with the Lord. (1 Thess. 4:16–17)

The Second Coming will be a day of great joy for the
righteous. For those who are caught up will embrace loved
ones who have come forth from their graves, and those who
have been prepared through sanctification to live upon the terrestrial earth.

> And the saints that are upon the earth, who are alive,
> shall be quickened and be caught up to meet him.
>
> And they who have slept in their graves shall come
> forth, for their graves shall be opened; and they also shall be
> caught up to meet him in the midst of the pillar of heaven—
> (D&C 88:96–97)

Nothing we can imagine will compare with the grandeur
of that occasion. Never again will weakness, pain and distress
be a part of our lives. Never again will the corruption of age
wage war upon our bodies or infirmities, sickness or the limitations of the flesh fetter us or keep us down. So many changes
will take place that the old earth, or our time upon it, will hardly
be remembered. The newly cleansed earth will at long last be

sanctified, beautified and prepared for the millennial family.

> The earth shall pass away. And there shall be a new heaven and a new earth: and they shall be like unto the old save the old have passed away, and all things have become new. (Ether 13:8-9)

Without the evil influence of the devil, and because of the earth's new glorified state, the seventh millennium will be the most glorious of all. The paradisiacal earth will be fruitful and her bountiful harvests will fill the land (Articles of Faith 10). Forests will tower over fruitful plains and streams will quench the thirst of barren lands. Lush vegetation will grow abundantly, and the thorn will be forever lost. Her fertile fields will be home to the righteous, and her rolling hills will be dotted with magnificent cities and temples. In her renewed state she will shine with great glory and will at long last be a fit abode for the Savior and those who are his at his coming. Thus, our valiant Mother Earth will rest at last from her labors and will enjoy a Sabbath of peace along with all those who abide the day.

~ ~ ~

Notes

1. Smith, *Teachings of the Prophet,* 253.
2. Ibid, 13.
3. Taylor, *Government of God,* 101, quoted in Lund, *Coming of the Lord,* 84.
4. Penrose, "Second Advent," 583, quoted in Lund, *Coming of the Lord,* 202.

Chapter Five

Who Shall Abide the Day?

And the LORD shall utter his voice before his army: for his camp is very great: for he is strong that executeth his word: for the day of the LORD is great and very terrible; and who can abide it? (Joel 2:11)

From the beginning of time the question has been asked, who shall abide the day of his coming? And the answer has always been the same. "He that hath clean hands, and a pure heart; who hath not lifted up his soul unto vanity, nor sworn deceitfully" (Ps 24:4). These are they who will be caught up to greet the Savior in the clouds of glory at the appointed hour—the honorable and decent of the world.

While it is true that the war between good and evil has been with us since the foundations of the earth were laid, and is escalating before our very eyes, we must not forget that numerous good and honorable people from all dispensations of time have lived out their days in righteousness. Although often surrounded by great wickedness, many of God's children remained true to the measure of light which was theirs to enjoy at the time and did not fall victim to the decadent enticings of Lucifer. Not all lived during a time when the gospel was available, but they lived lives of honor nonetheless, and did the best they could to be decent human beings in spite of the fact that Lucifer was trying his best to corrupt mankind. Thus, although his success rate is high, Satan has not won the war yet, nor will he ever.

~ ~ ~

Before the world was created Lucifer desired the throne of God and to deny men of their agency. For that reason he was cast out of heaven and sent to earth where he and his followers have been busily engaged in the warfare with the righteous ever since. He is absolutely ruthless in his war upon the god-fearing. Where he cannot always tempt them by more traditional means, he simply leads them into the valley of contentment where he can catch them in those snares he has carefully placed in their path to entrap them when they are at their most vulnerable. As the rabbit sees only the morsel of food in the trap, and never the trap, all too often the weary hearted see only the pleasant tidbit placed before them, and neglect to see, or feel, or discern the terrible ramifications which could result from nibbling on such tasty delights. The adversary knows that those who indulge themselves in his feasts of perversion, and persistently neglect the word of God, soon learn to love darkness more than light.

Satan is perfectly aware that those of this generation are overworked, underpaid, and often stressed to the very limits of their endurance. He also knows that many often feel too busy with the struggles of life to search the scriptures daily. Thus, he spreads a feast of deceit before them that is enticing. He provides easy answers to their questions and a plan of self indulgence which has deadly consequences. Unfortunately, those who fall into this diabolical trap soon become intoxicated with such pride and selfishness that they begin to look *inward* for their needs rather than *upward* toward God. Moreover, they become so intent on satisfying their own selfish desires that they no longer feel inclined to succor the needs of others or to serve country, neighbor or home. Therefore, we must be constantly on guard against his plan for our souls and the downfall of our country—indeed the world. Fighting him can only be done on a personal basis. This is a one-on-one war. But, it will be the combined efforts of many righteous Saints that will eventually defeat him. Only by personal righteousness and by putting on the full armor of God can we fight this insidious battle. Therefore, we must hold onto the iron rod more tightly than we ever dreamed we could, for our lives are in more peril from the demons of hell than by any famine, flood or earthquake. If such disasters take our lives while holding true to our faith, our inheritance is assured, but if we fall victim to the enticings of the devil, we may be everlastingly lost. In spite of such ominous warnings, however, the righteous need not fear, for the wicked will soon be wiped away and those who abide the day will enjoy a millennium of peace.

> For in mine own due time will I come upon the earth in judgement, and my people shall be redeemed and shall reign with me on earth.
>
> For the great Millennium, of which I have spoken by the mouth of my servants, shall come. (D&C 43:29–30)

Only by vigilance and by putting on the full armor of God will we be able to abide the day, however, for the world has become a place of distorted truths and corrupt beliefs. It is filled with deception and bigotry. Thus, our first and foremost responsibility to ourselves and to our families is to learn what truth is and where to find it. The beautiful example of the Savior's life gives us a firm foundation to build upon. By living the design he has given us for happy productive lives, we can find reassurance that our chosen path is correct and that our footing is sure. Yet, we must build upon that foundation by study and prayer if we are to understand more fully the plan of salvation and our duties toward God. We must pursue a course which will lead us to exaltation, and then follow that course until the end of our days. Endurance becomes a key word and will take us up the long road toward perfection and ultimately into the presence of the Father.

It is also imperative that we study the word of God dur-

ing these trying times, for the scriptures give us ample counsel concerning our place in the scheme of things and our mode
of action in this war between good and evil. There will never
come a time when having a testimony is of more value to us
than it is today or when that testimony needs to be as strong or
self supporting.

> A gracious God, who does all things well and is him-
> self all powerful, all wise, and all knowing, reveals his mind
> and will to men so they can advance and progress and become
> like him. He gives his doctrines to men so they will know
> what to believe and what to do to gain eternal life. All doc-
> trine—all gospel concepts of every sort and nature—all are
> revealed and preached to prepare men for celestial rest. And
> we have no better illustration of this than the doctrine of the
> second coming of the Son of Man. One of the chief reasons
> this doctrine is revealed is to teach us what we must do,
> whether in life or in death, to abide the day.[1]

Not only has the Lord provided us with scriptures which
impart his will to mankind, but he has also provided prophets
to receive instruction in our behalf and to give council when
needed. He has declared his will to his children from the earliest of days—study his word, listen to his prophets, pray daily,
teach your children, walk in honorable paths and keep his
commandments. The same message is repeated over and over
again—no one can miss it.

> Pray always, that you may come off conqueror; yea,
> that you may conquer Satan, and that you may escape the
> hands of the servants of Satan that do uphold his work.
> (D&C 10:5)

At this eleventh hour it is absolutely critical that we be
steadfast in the faith, that we might not be deceived by the
countless false messages and miracles that come from the father
of lies. His resources are endless and his power greater than
we know. He can chip away at an individual or a family so quietly and insidiously that they often fall without a whimper of

protest. Moreover, by destroying the family he knows he can gain control of an entire nation, for the family is the very foundation of strength upon which every nation grows and prospers. His plan both begins and ends by tempting men away from God and then by slowly and systematically chipping away at the principles of decency which knit together a family or society. He continues by teasing their minds with enticements of more power and more wealth. He further admonishes them to seek it now and to seek it at any price.

Sadly, there seems to be no tomorrow in the realm of today's reality. We must enjoy "now" the wealth, power or fame which took our parents and forefathers a lifetime to acquire. The need for cars that feed the egos and the homes which advertise status has driven many families beyond their means and women from the home and into the workplace. Yet, in our quest for the things of the world we pay a dear price. With the new houses, cars, clothes, and luxurious vacations comes a generation of children who have been emotionally and sometimes physically abandoned and who lack the security and self esteem to become part of a happy and well-adjusted adult population. The lost children of this last generation are so filled with rage that growing numbers are taking to the streets, some in open rebellion against the laws of the land, and others simply in hopes of finding the security and love they find so lacking in their own homes. There is a loss of discipline in every school and home in the nation as well as around the world. The waywardness which generally occurs in the adolescent society has not just doubled or tripled in the last few decades, but is now the norm.

We cannot help but sorrow for the lost values and the corrupted standards of conduct which have spawned such a world of wretchedness. We try hard to hold our families together in spite of it all, but we must do more. We must prepare our homes with strength that can come only from prayer, study and faith. We must nourish honorable standards of conduct and avoid the popular fads of the day. We must remind ourselves that God's plan for his children is a good one, and that the Saints are richly blessed—even in the midst of such chaos. We must rekindle the old fashioned standards which made our country great, for far too many of our time-honored disciplines have become distant memories. The work ethics which made our forefathers strong are becoming a thing of the past, and more and more seek for gain without pain. Pride in one's craft has lost ground to the dog-eat-dog ideology which propels men and women through the ranks of business and into the dizzying pace of the elite rich. The spirit of speculation has replaced the stabilizing influence of the solid ventures. The need to acquire more and more of the world's possessions has clouded our minds and caused us to forget our purpose for this sojourn in mortality—to grow, to love, to serve, to perfect ourselves and to prepare to meet God.

~ ~ ~

Since the first day of creation, darkness has tried to rule over light. But we must never forget that Christ is the chief light giver in the world, and if we follow his example and his admonition to love and serve one another, we can successfully keep the light burning in the hearts of the valiant until the Savior's triumphant return when darkness and death will at long last be replaced by light and life eternal.

In his instructions to the Nephites Jesus said, "Behold, I am the light which ye shall hold up—that which ye have seen me do." (3 Ne. 18:24) The Lord has called upon each of us to be not only our brother's keeper, but to join with him as keepers of the light as well. He has admonished us to let our lights so shine that our good works can be seen, that the Father might be glorified.

The Prophet Joseph Smith and so many others throughout past generations read the Bible by the light of a single candle. The truths that fed their souls were glorious, and the message of hope they found had the power to change their lives. Likewise, our lights may seem small and insignificant when compared with some of the more gifted theologians of our day, but our light, nonetheless, coupled with the light of many others can have a profound effect on a hungry soul. Our small light can often light the way in another's dark world or lead us through a troubled night or a day of sorrow. Together, each with a single flame, the family of man could create a blaze which could light up the heavens. And, by loving one another and succoring each other's needs, we could finally become a Zion people, fully prepared for the Savior's triumphant return.

The heavenly inspired Golden Rule has guided many a youngster's step, and could well be the formula which would bring the world into peaceful cohabitation. "And as ye would that men should do to you, do ye also to them likewise" (Luke 6:31). Would we be inclined to rob another of their personal treasures if we were to put ourselves in the role of the robbed? Would we injure or cause harm if we could feel the pains of the injured? Would we bear false witness if we could feel the anger of the unjustly accused. Would we be inclined to gossip if we could feel the embarrassment of sins made public? Would we mame or kill or seek injury to any other if we could truly feel as they feel, cry as they cry, sorrow as they sorrow? This one principle could do more good in the world than man can imagine, but alas, the tempter would have us believe that man is an entity to himself and should not be compelled to be his brother's keeper. He would have us believe that we must strike first lest the enemy be upon us. Entire governments have been overthrown by despicable men whose lust for power overrode any concern they had for the welfare of the vast populations whose lives would be altered by their actions. Could such a thing happen if we were to love our neighbor as ourselves and spend our time and talents in the pursuit of a Zion-oriented society—a society where everyone is indeed his brother's keeper and the happiness of those around us is as important to us as our own? Why is it that the simplicity of it all eludes us, and we continue to search for the answers to a utopian society by searching various man-made blueprints? Only God in his great and all-encompassing wisdom can come up with a formula that would end the ills of the world and lead us into a society of peace, and has done so, yet the world continues to resist. We, then, must seek peace in a more restricted arena. As we would not plant flowers in a weed patch, we too, must be cautious of the environment we choose for ourselves and our families. For as the blossoms would be choked out by the weeds which spread so rapidly through the garden, so will we be influenced by the environment we choose to live in. There are many weeds in the world—weeds and briars which choke out the goodness and respect we are trying to foster in our lives. Being armed with righteousness is not always enough if we deliberately place ourselves in harm's way.

There is a saying which teaches us that "likes attract." Evil doers seek out their own kind as do those who are more righteous. To be safe in the bosom of friends and family who espouse the same belief system and moral standards is a great protection and can afford us a measure of security in an otherwise uncertain world. As you would not permit your children to play with the ruffians in the street, so we should keep our lives unspotted from the world and secure for ourselves those friends and activities which meet the standards consistent with Christian living. We must keep our feet firmly planted on the straight and narrow path and avoid the many detours which would lead us astray or into those mists of darkness that blind the eye and make us prime candidates for temptation or sin.

Satan and his demonic angels seek to destroy the righteous and often appear in sheep's clothing, but by listening to the promptings of the Holy Ghost we can often detect the wolf which lurks beneath. Nothing is of more importance in our present day and age than learning to live by the Spirit. To be recipients of inspiration and guidance is imperative lest we fall victim to the many diabolical schemes the devil has ordained for the destruction of man.

How then, can we safeguard ourselves and our families? The answer lies in the many sermons and lessons taught by the Savior, and by holding fast to the iron rod.

> And it came to pass that I beheld that the rod of iron, which my father had seen, was the word of God, which led to the fountain of living waters, or to the tree of life; which waters are a representation of the love of God; and I also beheld that the tree of life was a representation of the love of God. (1 Ne. 11:25)

The Savior tells us to pray, lest we enter into temptation, and instructs us further that we must obey his commandments that we might be worthy of his blessings. He also instructs us to give compassionate service to others and to be honest in all our dealings with our fellow man. We are taught to love all men regardless of race or station and, as hard as it might be, to forgive those who despitefully use us. We must give alms to the poor and serve in the kingdom as strength permits. We must avoid pride and try at all times to keep ourselves unspotted from the world.

> Pride goeth before destruction, and an haughty spirit before a fall. (Prov. 16:18)

Although such instructions seem simple, they can at times be overwhelming to the heart that cries out from the pain of injustice or abuse. Therefore, the protection we seek must go beyond the protection of our mortal tabernacle—it is an eternal safety net we seek. The pure in heart—those who still love and serve in the face of impossible odds and overcome the trials of mortality with dignity and without an overabundance of murmuring—are the ones who will inherit the earth and find their way into the mansions of our Heavenly Father. Thus, it is our characters that need safeguarding and our determination to do right in an angry world. It is our love for our Savior and our desire to overcome, as did he, that will propel us upward and onward through the mists of darkness and despair which make up so much of our mortal experience. These qualities of heart will bring honor to our name both in this world and the next. No matter what else we do, we must be true to ourselves and our God and plant seeds of love and kindness within our hearts that will grow and flourish and make us fit recipients for the glories of eternal life.

Our safety lies in living each day as though the Savior were walking beside us and choosing our actions accordingly. If we follow closely in the footsteps he has left behind, we can surely find our way in a world that seems bleak and unfeeling and can gather strength from his holy presence. Above all, however, we must always remember that he is a God, and we should honor the decisions he and our Heavenly Father have made in regard to our mortal schooling—regardless of our liking or even understanding them. Truly they can see a bigger picture than we can. Our trials are for our eternal good and often it is only after a trial that we discover a new strength or a hidden talent.

> Let your hearts be comforted concerning Zion; for all flesh is in mine hands; *be still and know that I am God.* (D&C 101:16; emphasis added)

As overwhelming as the prophecies of the last days seem to be when we read them all at once, we must always remember that God is at the helm and directing the work at hand. Moreover, he has promised that he will strengthen us against the coming days and will provide the means, if we are righteous, to survive the calamities of the last days. In fact, as unlikely as it seems, we will probably spend most of our remaining years going about our business just as we always have. This is made more understandable if we remember that just before the each new year is ushered in, it seems each TV network gathers all the bad news of that past year together, and in a brief segment of two or three minutes, lets it pass quickly before our eyes. We sit in horror and wonder how we survived it all. But during that same year babies were born and marriages took place. We went to school and to work. We sang, laughed, cried and played. We enjoyed Christmas and holidays, bought new clothes or cars or toys and enjoyed them. We went on vacations, painted the house, were sick a time or two and got well. We changed jobs or went to college, visited relatives and even went through the death and burial of loved ones. In other words—life went on, and so will we!

The righteous of today were chosen from the billions of God's children to come to earth during this terrible time of upheaval. Moreover, they have been given the charge to help in the gathering of Israel from the four corners of the earth and in establishing Zion in preparation for the Savior's triumphant return. These are major undertakings and there are perils all around us. Yet the assurance that God is directing the work of the last days personally should give us comfort and the strength to trudge forward through unlit paths and complete the task at hand. We cannot give up the fight when the victory is so close. Thus, we must gird up our loins and endure whatever trials come our way, confident in the knowledge that the dawn of a new day is at our very doors. Peace will soon come and the tears of sorrow which our mortal experience has thrust upon us will be remembered no more. An eternal happiness awaits the righteous which will be more glorious than anything we can imagine, and at long last we will understand why we were called upon to endure so much. Truly, the faithful need not fear.

> Who among us shall dwell with the devouring fire?
> who among us shall dwell with everlasting burnings?
>
> He that walketh righteously, and speaketh uprightly;
> he that despiseth the gain of oppressions, that shaketh his
> hands from holding of bribes, that stoppeth his ears from

hearing of blood, and shutteth his eyes from seeing evil;
(Isa. 33:14–15)

The wicked sometimes foolishly suppose that they, too, will be rewarded with the same reward as the righteous. But, they are mistaken.

> And now we call the proud happy; yea, they that work wickedness are set up; yea, they that tempt God are even delivered.
>
> Then they that feared the Lord spake often one to another, and the Lord hearkened and heard; and a book of remembrance was written before him for them that feared the Lord, and that thought upon his name.
>
> And they shall be mine, saith the Lord of Hosts, in that day when I make up my jewels; and I will spare them as a man spareth his own son that serveth him.
>
> Then shall ye return and discern between the righteous and the wicked, between him that serveth God and him that serveth him not. (3 Ne. 24:15–18)

Who shall abide the burning? The pure in heart, the valiant, the honorable and decent of the world; those who maintain their more noble characteristics in spite of Lucifer's incessant attacks upon righteousness; those who do not entangle themselves in corrupt behavior and fall victim to deceitful practices; those who let love and goodness govern their thoughts and actions and those who love God.

> Abide ye in the liberty wherewith ye are made free; entangle not yourselves in sin, but let your hands be clean, until the Lord comes. (D&C 88:86)

Such simple instructions. *Let your hands be clean until the Lord comes.* Once again we must remember that the laws of God were instigated for *our* benefit and for *our* ultimate good. Only by learning to live by God's laws can we hope to be a part of his society and enjoy the companionship of an eternal celestial family. Thus, the only sure safeguard we have against Satan's influence is to follow the Savior's admonition to be clean through and through, for as sure as the day follows the night, those who indulge themselves in sin and follow after worldly pursuits will perish in the end. Today, then, is the day we must be concerned about, a day when evil is at our very doors; a day when we must be about our Father's business in helping roll the kingdom along.

> Behold, now it is called today until the coming of the Son of Man, and verily it is a day of sacrifice, and a day for the tithing of my people; for he that is tithed shall not be burned at his coming.
>
> For after today cometh the burning—this is speaking after the manner of the Lord—for verily I say, tomorrow all the proud and they that do wickedly shall be as stubble; and I will burn them up, for I am the Lord of Hosts; and I will not spare any that remain in Babylon.
>
> Wherefore, if ye believe me, ye will labor while it is called today. (D&C 64:23–25)

Thus only those who remain true and faithful on a daily basis will be caught up to greet the Savior when he comes in all his glory to claim the kingdoms of the world. Gratefully, our efforts to remain pure in spite of tribulations of these last frightening days will not be in vain, for a new world awaits the faithful which will be more glorious than anything we ever imagined; a world of peace, joy and happiness. Therefore, rejoice! The Lord is King, and the heavens and all the holy angels are preparing for his reign as King of Kings and Lord of Lords over the whole earth and everything in it.

~ ~ ~

Note

1. McConkie, *Millennial Messiah*, 538.

Chapter Six

The Transfigured Earth

And my people shall dwell in a peaceable habi-
tation, and in sure dwellings, and in quiet resting
places. (Isa. 32:18)

As with man, the earth is in the process of being sanctified. She was first created spiritually, then temporally. She
underwent a baptism at the time of Noah's flood and will ultimately be baptized with fire at the Savior's coming. She trans-
gressed not the law and has thus filled the measure of her
creation. Soon we will witness her death song, and will all but
feel her pain as she reels to and fro and struggles through her
last few years of existence in her telestial state. When at long
last the Savior comes, his mighty voice alone will cause great
changes to come upon her.

> And it shall be a voice as the voice of many waters,
> and as the voice of a great thunder, which shall break down
> the mountains, and the valleys shall not be found.
>
> He shall command the great deep, and it shall be driven
> back into the north countries, and the islands shall become
> one land;
>
> And the land of Jerusalem and the land of Zion shall
> be turned back into their own place, and the earth shall be
> like as it was in the days before it was divided. (D&C
> 133:22–24)

In Isaiah we learn that the earth will actually be moved
out of its place at the Savior's coming.

> The earth is utterly broken down, the earth is clean dissolved, the earth is moved exceedingly.
>
> The earth shall reel to and fro like a drunkard, and shall be removed like a cottage; and the transgression thereof shall be heavy upon it; and it shall fall, and not rise again. (Isa. 24:19–20)

Such mighty changes will take place at the time of the Second Advent that the earth will be totally transfigured. "Every valley shall be exalted, and every mountain and hill shall be made low: and the crooked shall be made straight, and the rough places plain" (Isa. 40:4). An entirely new heaven and earth will come into existence and Mother Earth will finally enjoy that beauty and grandeur she knew so long ago in the Garden of Eden.

> For, behold, I create new heavens and a new earth: and the former shall not be remembered, nor come into mind. (Isa. 65:17)

At long last, the corruptible things of the earth will be forgotten and once again the earth will be returned to a state of paradise. Deserts will become gardens, and rivers, streams, and fresh water pools will replace parched ground. Flowers will bloom spontaneously and magnificent trees will dot the land, and the earth will finally rest from her labors and enjoy a Sabbath of peace.

With the earth restored to its paradisiacal glory, the Savior, along with numerous resurrected saints such as Adam, Enoch, Abraham, Isaac, Jacob, Lehi, Nephi, Moroni and others—as well as all those righteous mortals who were caught up before the fiery wrath of his indignation cleansed the world—will descend with him to usher in the Millennium. How wonderful it will be to mingle with the righteous saints from all dispensations of time—those who remained faithful to their covenants, who prayed and fasted and bore testimony of the divine nature of the Savior. At long last the rewards of the faithful will be realized and those who endured the hardships of mortality will come to realize that nothing was too great a price to pay for the rewards they were now to enjoy.

~ ~ ~

When the earth was first formed, the Creators stood back and declared that it was "good," for beauty was everywhere. Although she ultimately fell from her paradisaical glory, Mother Earth continued to be blessed with great beauty. Even in the most barren desert the cactus flower turned its face toward God and brightened its surroundings. Throughout the long ages of history, travelers from all lands have noted the wonders they encountered in their various journeys. Descriptions were given of the lush and fertile valleys of the Nile in Egypt and of the beautiful waterways in Persia. The exotic valleys and plains of the Orient are legendary as well as the lush green countrysides of Europe and Asia. Truly, even in her fallen state, the earth has always been cloaked in majesty.

The Hawaiian Islands, with their towering canopies and tropical splendor, probably come as close to Eden as we mere mortals can imagine, but the original Garden of Eden was located in Jackson County, Missouri, according to the Prophet Joseph Smith (see *Journal of Discourses,* 11:337), a place that still greets the eye with indescribable beauty. Brigham Young said:

> Now it is a pleasant thing to think of and to know where the garden of Eden was. . . in Jackson County was the garden of Eden. Joseph has declared this, and I am as much bound to believe that as to believe that Joseph was a prophet of God.[1]

Can we wonder then why Jackson Country, Missouri, was chosen as the place of the New Jerusalem? Even today that sacred region greets the eye with unbelievable beauty. The Prophet Joseph Smith describes his view of that area in these words:

As far as the eye can reach the beautiful rolling prairies spread out like a sea of meadows, and are decorated with a growth of flowers so gorgeous and grand as to exceed description; and nothing is more fruitful or a richer stockholder in the blooming prairie than the honey bee. Only on the water courses is timber to be found. There, in strips from one to three miles in width, and following faithfully the meanderings of the stream, it grows in luxuriant forests. The forests are a mixture of oak, hickory, black, walnut, elm, ash, cherry, honey locust, mulberry, coffee bean, hackberry, box elder, and basswood; with the addition of cottonwood, butterwood, pecan, and soft and hard maple upon the bottoms. The shrubbery is beautiful and consists of plums, grapes, crab apple, and persimmons.

The soil is rich and fertile; from three to ten feet deep, and generally composed of a rich black mold, intermingled with clay and sand. It yields in abundance. Buffalo, elk, deer, bear, wolves, beaver and many smaller animals here roam at pleasure. Turkeys, geese, swans, duck, and a variety of the feathered tribe, are among the rich abundance that grace the delightful regions of this goodly land.[2]

If these beautiful temporal scenes delight our senses and give us joy, we can only imagine what beauty awaits us in the Millennium, for the earth will once again be paradisiacal in nature, a terrestrial sphere (A of F 10). We might remember the telestial glory is compared to the stars in the firmament while the terrestrial is compared to that of the moon (see D&C 76:78–81). With that comparison before us, we can only imagine the beauty that awaits us when the earth becomes a global Garden of Eden filled with both flora and fauna of every description. We can imagine flowers that bloom spontaneously, flowers of magnificent beauty and colors of every hue, or perhaps meadows ablaze with dazzling blossoms which dance in the afternoon breeze. We can visualize broad grasslands and sweeping prairies and an infinite variety of trees gracing emerald green forests, each providing fruit and nutmeats for the taking. Freshwater lakes, ponds, streams and waterfalls will undoubtedly dot the landscape and the cry of the loon and other waterfowl will be heard across the land. A vast variety of birds will sing their songs, and even the soft murmerings of insects will please the ear. Yet, without a doubt, anything our finite minds can imagine will pale in comparison to the glorious scenes that await us.

> For the LORD shall comfort Zion: he will comfort all her waste places; and he will make her wilderness like Eden, and her desert like the garden of the LORD; joy and gladness shall be found therein, thanksgiving, and the voice of melody. (Isa. 51:3)

~ ~ ~

Other great blessings await us as well. As a terrestrial order comes into existence, man and beast will interact peacefully for the first time since Adam and Eve walked the Garden of Eden. Animals of every kind and description will roam the land without the least concern for their safety and vegetation will sustain them. The otter will play in the stream unafraid while the jackal and deer will run together in peace. All animosity between man and beast will at long last and forever be done away with during the great Day of the Lord.

> The wolf also shall dwell with the lamb, and the leopard shall lie down with the kid; and the calf and the young lion and the fatling together; and a little child shall lead them.
>
> And the cow and the bear shall feed; their young ones shall lie down together; and the lion shall eat straw like the ox.
>
> And the suckling child shall play on the hole of the asp, and the weaned child shall put his hand on the cockatrice's den.
>
> They shall not hurt nor destroy in all my holy mountain; for the earth shall be full of the knowledge of the LORD, as the waters cover the sea. (Isa. 11:6–9)

What a wonderful time to live. To be able to mingle with various beasts and enjoying their companionship is an exciting concept. Their gentle natures and their intelligence and beauty will be magnified, and man will be able to interact with them peacefully and without fear of any kind.

Many have wondered about animals in the overall scheme of things. Will they too be exalted? We learn in the Doctrine and Covenants that immortality extends to all forms of life:

> For all old things shall pass away, and all things shall become new, even the heaven and the earth, both men and beasts, the fowls of the air, and the fishes of the sea;
>
> And not one hair, neither mote, shall be lost, for it is the workmanship of mine hand. (D&C 29:24–25)

Joseph Smith gives us further insight into this matter as he interprets John's vision of heaven:

> I suppose John saw beings there of a thousand forms, that had been saved from ten thousand times ten thousand earths like this,—strange beasts of which we have no conception: All might be seen in heaven. The grand secret was to show John what there was in heaven. "I John learned that God glorified Himself by saving all that His hands had made, whether beasts, fowls, fishes or men; and He will glorify Himself with them."
>
> Says one, "I cannot believe in the salvation of beasts." Any man who would tell you that this could not be, would tell you that the revelations are not true. John heard the words of the beasts giving glory to God, and understood them. God who made the beasts could understand every language spoken by them. The four beasts were four of the most noble animals that had filled the measure of their creation, and had been saved from other worlds, because they were perfect: they were like angels in their sphere. We are not told where they came from and I do not know; but they were seen and heard by John praising and glorifying God.[3]

Through all the generations of time, Mother Nature has required the flesh of one animal to sustain another. This great food chain has been in operation since the fall of Adam. But, when the Millennium arrives, the animosity which exists between various animals in this life will depart, and the entire animal kingdom will mingle together in peace. Thus, in some miraculous way, life as we know it will cease and flesh will no longer feed upon flesh. Trees will no longer die their seasonal deaths only to be renewed again in springtime but will bear their fruit continually. Vast plains covered with lush vegetation will beautify the land and replace the jagged unproductive mountains ranges that were thrown up during the travail of Mother Earth. Hurricanes, tornados and violent storms will be a thing of the past, and rain will fall as a gentle mist upon the ground.

Man, too, will enjoy a new state of contentment. His anger, pride and carnal nature will be replaced with his more noble characteristics, and, in his renewed state, will love God and righteousness. To add to this happy state, that old serpent, the devil, will at long last be bound and will cease to plague mankind.

Now, Satan's ability to tempt man has always, and will always be conditional on man's own invitation. Yet, with the Spirit of God permeating the earth in such rich abundance during the Millennium, men's hearts will be turned away from every evil thought. Thus, Satan will be bound by their righteousness until the thousand years is ended. The scriptures teach us:

> And because of the righteousness of his people, Satan has no power; wherefore, he cannot be loosed for the space of many years; for he hath no power over the hearts of the people, for they dwell in righteousness, and the Holy One of Israel reigneth. (1 Ne. 22:26)

In our premortal existence, Lucifer stood in rank as one of the great ones. He possessed highly developed intelligence and qualities of leadership which drew many after him.

> And this we saw also, and bear record, that an angel of God who was in authority in the presence of God, who rebelled against the Only Begotten Son whom the Father loved and who was in the bosom of the Father, was thrust down from the presence of God and the Son.

> And was called Perdition, for the heavens wept over him—he was Lucifer, a son of the morning.
>
> And we beheld, and lo, he is fallen! is fallen, even a son of the morning! (D&C 76:25–27)

How could so great a man fall from such a lofty station, and how could so many follow after him, even a third part of Father's children? (Rev. 12:4) The heavens wept for the loss. Sadly, his lust for power overcame him and ultimately cost him everything. That same desire for power and glory motivates his actions today. But, the day of his power is growing shorter, and soon he will be shackled for nearly a thousand years. So great will be his fall that men will look at him in astonishment and wonder amongst themselves how he gained such control over the hearts of so many throughout the ages.

> How art thou fallen from heaven, O Lucifer, son of the morning! How art thou cut down to the ground, which didst weaken the nations!
>
> For thou hast said in thine heart, I will ascend into heaven, I will exalt my throne above the stars of God: I will sit also upon the mount of the congregation, in the sides of the north:
>
> I will ascend above the heights of the clouds; I will be like the most High.
>
> Yet thou shalt be brought down to hell, to the sides of the pit.
>
> They that see thee shall narrowly look upon thee, and consider thee, saying, is this the man that made the earth to tremble, that did shake kingdoms;
>
> That made the world as a wilderness, and destroyed the cities thereof; that opened not the house of his prisoners?
>
> All the kings of the nations even all of them, lie in glory, every one in his own house,
>
> But thou art cast out of thy grave like an abominable branch, and as the raiment of those that are slain, thrust through with a sword, that go down to the stones of the pit; as a carcass trodden under feet. (Isa. 14:12–19)

Although it is exciting to contemplate what earth life will be like without the evil influence of Satan nipping at our heels, Brigham Young teaches us that Satan and his evil influence was a necessary part of our mortal experience (D&C 29:39).

> Sin has come into the world, and death by sin. I frequently ask myself the question: was there any necessity for sin to enter the world? Most assuredly there was, according to my understanding and reasoning powers. Did I not know the evil I could never know the good; had I not seen the light I should never be able to comprehend what darkness is. Had I never tried to see and behold a thing in darkness I could not understand the beauty and glory of the light. If I had never tasted the bitter or the sour how could I define or describe the sweet.[3]

> Sin is in the world, but it is not necessary that we should sin, because sin is in the world; but, to the contrary, it is necessary that we should resist sin and for this purpose is sin necessary. Sin exists in all the eternities. Sin is co-eternal with righteousness, for it must needs be that there is an opposition in all things.[4]

Our mortal condition is filled with all the trials and blessing needed for man to experience joy, pain, sorrow, gladness, despair, and happiness—experiences which help us refine ourselves and help to perfect us. Untold experiences in the premortal world also played a part. Many of those experiences helped to shape our character and personality and came with us into mortality. Thus, while in our mortal condition we can either choose to develop and refine our more noble characteristics, or let our baser more worldly selves become the dominant force in our life. Whichever we choose, that same character will go with us into the next life (Alma 34:34). Thus, in spite of their glorious surroundings, man will still struggle with decisions and need to develop those skills designed to bring him happiness—the great difference being that Satan will no longer be among them. If, then, man still chooses to sin by virtue of his agency, it will be because of his own will and not because of the enticements of Lucifer. Nonetheless, the task of perfecting one's self will be much easier, for the Light of Christ will permeate the entire world during the great Sabbath of time. There will be no murders or theft of any kind nor any lying, jealousy, or pride. Man will delight in good works and will seek to strengthen his brethren. His capacity to love will fill his whole being and charity will rule his thoughts continually. Nonetheless, his agency will remain. But, with the enlightenment of his mind, body and senses, he will understand all things more perfectly.

~ ~ ~

Perhaps one of the greatest changes to take place during the Millennium will be the change from our mortal condition to that of a resurrected being in the twinkling of an eye.

> And there shall be no sorrow because there is no death.
>
> In that day an infant shall not die until he is old; and his life shall be as the age of a tree;
>
> And when he dies he shall not sleep, that is to say in the earth, but shall be changed in the twinkling of an eye, and shall be caught up, and his rest shall be glorious. (D&C 101:29–31)

Man's capacity to learn will also be heightened during the Millennium and he will delight in searching out those mysteries which have confounded mankind since the beginning of time.

> God shall give unto you knowledge by his Holy Spirit, yea, by the unspeakable gift of the Holy Ghost, that has not been revealed since the world was until now;
>
> Which our forefathers have awaited with anxious expectation to be revealed in the last times, which their minds were pointed to by the angels, as held in reserve for the fulness of their glory;

> A time to come in the which nothing shall be with-
> held, whether there be one God or many gods, they shall be
> manifest.
>
> All thrones and dominions, principalities and powers,
> shall be revealed and set forth upon all who have endured
> valiantly for the gospel of Jesus Christ.
>
> And also, if there be bounds set to the heavens or to
> the seas, or to the dry land, or to the sun, moon, or stars—
>
> All the times of their revolutions; all the appointed
> days, months, and years, and all the days of their days,
> months, and years, and all their glories, laws, and set times,
> shall be revealed in the days of the dispensation of the ful-
> ness of times.(D&C 121: 26–31)

He will be taught by heavenly beings and Jesus Christ
himself will preach sermons never heard before. Our hearts
will leap with joy at the marvelous revelations which will
come forth at that time.

> Yea, verily I say unto you, in that day when the Lord
> shall come, he shall reveal all things—
>
> Things which have passed, and hidden things which
> no man knew, things of the earth, by which it was made, and
> the purpose and the end thereof—
>
> Things most precious, things that are above, and
> things that are beneath, things that are in the earth, and upon
> the earth, and in heaven. (D&C 101:32–34)

Christ will impart all wisdom and knowledge to those
who thirst. If a man asks, it will be given him and nothing shall
be withheld.

> For since the beginning of the world men have not
> heard, nor perceived by the ear, neither hath the eye seen, O
> God, beside thee, what he hath prepared for him that wait-
> eth for him. (Isa. 64:4)

The Sabbath of time will be the grandest of all the millenniums and man will produce more good works, more enlightened thought, more beautiful edifices, grand cities, magnificent

artworks and splendid music than we ever dreamed possible. Nothing our minds can imagine will compare with the beauty and glory that await the faithful during the great day of the Lord.

~ ~ ~

Notes

1. Brigham Young, in Journal History of the Church, March 15, 1857.

2. Smith, *History of the Church,* 1:197.

3. Smith, *Teachings of the Prophet,* 291.

4. Brigham Young, *Journal of Discourses,* 11:240.

Chapter Seven

Thy Kingdom Come

*O clap your hands, all ye people; shout unto God
with the voice of triumph.*
*For the Lord most high is terrible; he is a great
King over all the earth. (Ps. 47:1–2)*

While great kingdoms have come and gone throughout
man's probationary state, when the earth is cleansed of all
unrighteousness and then sanctified, the great Jehovah will
descend upon the new terrestrial earth and will set up a kingdom that will never be thrown down.

> And in the days of these kings shall the God of heaven
> set up a kingdom, which shall never be destroyed: and the
> kingdom shall not be left to other people, but it shall break
> in pieces and consume all these kingdoms, and it shall stand
> for ever. (Dan. 2:44)

As the righteous remnants of mankind begin their sojourn
through the Millennium, all men everywhere will accept Jesus
Christ as the rightful heir to the throne of David. Every ear will
hear and every knee will bow before him as he begins his reign
as Lord of Lords and King of Kings over the earth and all her
inhabitants. All nations will come to him for judgment, council and direction, and there will be peace upon the earth and in
the hearts of men. Brigham Young gives us further insights into
what the world will be like when the Savior takes possession
of his kingdom.

When the world is in a state of true civilization, man will have ceased to contend against his fellow-man, either as individuals, parties, communities, sects, or nations. This state of civilization will be brought about by the holy Priesthood of the Son of God; and men with full purpose of heart, will seek unto him who is pure and holy even our great Creator—our Father and God; and he will give them a law that is pure—a government and plan of society possessed by holy beings in heaven. Then there will be no more war, no more bloodshed, no more evil-speaking and evil-doing; but all will be contented to follow in the path of truth, which alone is calculated to exalt and dignify the whole man, mentally and physically, in all his operations, labors, and purposes.[1]

The keys and direction for that temple-oriented society were given to the Prophet Joseph Smith, in the Kirtland Temple, in 1836. The Lord declared that these manifestations and gifts were but the "beginnings of the blessings which shall be poured out upon the heads of my people" (D&C 110:10). Joseph Smith considered that day to be one of the greatest in all of history, for that outpouring opened the way for the restoration of all things.

Truly this is a day long to be remembered by the Saints of the last days,—a day in which the God of heaven has begun to restore the ancient order of His kingdom unto His servants and His people, a day in which all things are concurring to bring about the completion of the fullness of the gospel, a fullness of the dispensation of dispensations, even the fullness of times; a day in which God has begun to make manifest and set in order in His church those things which have been, and those things which the ancient prophets and wise men desired to see but died without beholding them; a day in which those things begin to be made manifest, which have been hid from before the foundation of the world, and which Jehovah has promised should be made known in His own due time unto His servants, to prepare the earth for the return of His glory even a celestial glory, and a kingdom of Priests and Kings to God and the Lamb, forever, on Mount Zion, and with him the hundred and forty and four thousand whom John the Revelator saw, all of which is to come to pass in the restitution of all things.[2]

Prophets proclaimed from the earliest of times that Christ would one day sit upon his throne and rule the world. The angel Gabriel carried that message to the young virgin Mary when he told her that she would conceive and bear the Son of God.

> He shall be great, and shall be called the Son of the Highest: and the Lord God shall give unto him the throne of his father David:
>
> And he shall reign over the house of Jacob for ever; and of his kingdom there shall be no end. (Luke 1:32–33)

During the Millennium, men will no longer live in fear of false judges or corrupt societies, for the Son of God will rule his kingdom in perfect righteousness. We learn from the Prophet Joseph Smith that the children of Israel were never happier than when the Lord was their lawgiver.

> When the children of Israel were chosen with Moses at their head, they were to be a peculiar people, among whom God should place His name; their motto was; "The Lord is our lawgiver; the Lord is our Judge; the Lord is our King, and He shall reign over us." While in this state they might truly say, "Happy is that people, whose God is the Lord," Their government was a theocracy; they had God to make their laws, and men chosen by Him to administer them; He was their God, and they were His people.[3]

Such will be the case in the Millennium, for he and he alone will rule the world. And, there should be no doubt that it is his right to rule, for he is the Creator and the means of salvation for all mankind. He is the great High Priest and the rightful heir, both temporally and spiritually, to the throne of David. Thus, it is his right alone to rule as King of Kings, Lord of Lords over the inhabitants of the whole earth.

> Jesus Christ, being the first Apostle thus commissioned, and the President of all the powers thus delegated,

is Lord of Lords, and King of Kings, in heaven and on the earth. Hence this Priesthood is called the Priesthood after the order of the Son of God. It holds the keys of all the true principles of government in all worlds, being without beginning of days or end of life. It . . . holds the keys of revelation of the oracles of God to man upon the earth; the power and right to give laws and commandments to individuals, churches, rulers, nations and the world; to appoint, ordain, and establish constitutions and kingdoms; to appoint kings, presidents, governors or judges, and to ordain or anoint them to their several holy callings, also to instruct, warn or reprove them by the word of the Lord.

It also holds the keys of the administration of ordinances for the remission of sins, and for the gift of the Holy Spirit; to heal the sick, cast out demons, or work miracles in the name of the Lord; in fine, to bind or loose on earth and in heaven.[4]

The time will soon be passed when wicked men will rule their religions by the sword and when the slaughter of millions will go on unopposed in the name of this god or that. The crusades of past ages and wars fought in the name of religion and so ordered by pious men who deluded themselves into thinking that God had ordained their actions, will no longer come into mind or be remembered. In God's society the needs of the people, both spiritually and temporally, will be met by a king who will serve his people with perfect love and will measure out justice in total and complete righteousness.

Although God introduced a pure form of government during the days of Adam and the early patriarchs ruled justly with their people, with the passing of time, the pure Adamic system was corrupted and cast aside by despicable men who sought for gain and power. Unfortunately, such perverted governments have been in place ever since. Thus God orchestrated the rise of a better government in these latter-days in America, to prepare men's hearts for the government of God which will be in full force during the Millennium. Brigham Young teaches us about how closely our own government resembles that ancient order.

> But few, if any, understand what a theocratic government is. In every sense of the word, it is a republican government, and differs but little in form from our National, State, and Territorial Government; but its subjects will recognize the will and dictation of the Almighty. . . .
>
> The Constitution and laws of the United States resemble a theocracy more closely than any government now on earth. . . . Even now the form of the Government of the United States differs but little from the Kingdom of God.[5]

President Young gives further insights into the part God played in the formation of our county's constitution and our way of life.

> The general Constitution of our country is good, and a wholesome government could be framed upon it, for it was dictated by the invisible operations of the Almighty; he moved upon Columbus to launch forth upon the trackless deep to discover the American Continent; he moved upon the signers of the Declaration of Independence; and he moved upon Washington to fight and conquer in the same way as he moved upon ancient and modern Prophets, each being inspired to accomplish the particular work he was called to perform in the times, seasons, and dispensations of the Almighty. God's purposes, in raising up these men and inspiring them with daring sufficient to surmount every opposing power, was to prepare the way for the formation of a true republican government. They laid its foundation; but when others came to build upon it, they reared a superstructure far short of their privileges, if they had walked uprightly as they should have done.[6]

He continues:

> We believe that the Lord has been preparing that when he should bring forth his work, that when the set time should fully come, there might be a place upon his footstool where sufficient liberty of conscience should exist, that his Saints might dwell in peace under the broad panoply of

87

constitutional law and equal rights. In this view we consider the men in the Revolution were inspired by the Almighty, to throw off the shackles of the mother government, with her established religion. For this cause were Adams, Jefferson, Franklin, Washington, and a host of others inspired to deeds of resistance to the acts of the King of Great Britain, who might also have been led to those aggressive acts, for aught we know, to bring to pass the purposes of God, in thus establishing a new government upon a principle of greater freedom, a basis of self-government allowing the free exercise of religious worship.

It was the voice of the Lord inspiring all those worthy men who bore influence in those trying times, not only to go forth in battle but to exercise wisdom in council, fortitude, courage, and endurance in the tented field, as well as subsequently to form and adopt those wise and efficient measures which secured to themselves and succeeding generations, the blessings of a free and independent government.

This government, so formed, has been blessed by the almighty until she spreads her sails in every sea, and her power is felt in every land.[7]

This divinely inspired government sheltered the religious pilgrims who came to her shores in search of religious freedom and set the stage for the restoration of the gospel which has since gone forth into all the world to gather the elect from the four corners of the world. Only in America where religious freedom flourishes could such a thing have happened. And it will be in this great country, a land foreordained as a land of liberty to its people from the earliest of times (see 2 Ne. 1:7) that the New Jerusalem will one day be built.

And behold, this people will I establish in this land, unto the fulfilling of the covenant which I made with your father Jacob; and it shall be a New Jerusalem. And the powers of heaven shall be in the midst of this people; yea, even I will be in the midst of you. (3 Ne. 20:22)

~ ~ ~

As part of his governing body, the Lord will restore judges, and the twelve apostles will be chief among them. The twelve disciples, who were with him during his sojourn in ancient America, will also be called to judge.

> And he said unto me: Thou rememberest the twelve apostles of the Lamb? Behold they are they who shall judge the twelve tribes of Israel; wherefore, the twelve ministers of thy seed shall be judged of them; for ye are of the house of Israel.
>
> And these twelve ministers whom thou beholdest shall judge thy seed. And, behold, they are righteous forever; for because of their faith in the Lamb of God their garments are made white in his blood. (1 Ne. 12:9–10)

The law will go forth from Zion to all the nations of the world, and will teach men everywhere how to live in peace. Judgements will come from those so commissioned from the ranks of the holy Priesthood, who will judge the peoples of the world with the pure love of Christ.

> When the judgment is given to the Saints, it will be because of their righteousness, because they will judge even as the angels and as the Gods, and not as the wicked do at the present time, who care not for God nor for justice, who care not for truth nor mercy, love nor kindness, who judge according to the wickedness of their hearts.[8]

Joseph Smith teaches us the formula whereby the priesthood will administer justice.

> No power or influence can or ought to be maintained by virtue of the priesthood, only by persuasion, by long suffering by gentleness and meekness, and by love unfeigned;
>
> By kindness, and pure knowledge which shall greatly enlarge the soul without hypocrisy and without guile. (D&C 121:41–42)

Although Christ will continue to have duties on both sides of the veil during the Millennium, he will dwell among

89

his people on the newly sanctified earth as often as is necessary to administer the affairs of his kingdom.

> But, verily I say unto you that in time ye shall have no King nor ruler, for I will be your king and watch over you.
>
> Wherefore, hear my voice and follow me, and you shall be a free people, and ye shall have no laws but my laws when I come, for I am your lawgiver, and what can stay my hand? (D&C 38:21–22)

~ ~ ~

When the kingdoms of the earth are finally united in one, a pure language will be restored so that all men will be able to communicate with one another with perfect ease. It will be that same language Father Adam was given in the Garden of Eden.

> For then will I turn to the people a pure language, that they may all call upon the name of the LORD, to serve him with one consent. (Zeph. 3:9)

Thus, at long last, all barriers of race and language will be done away with. The perfected kingdom will be a divine patriarchal order and will incorporate all functions of both church and state. It will become, in its perfected state, the Church of the Firstborn. Under this order, honorable men will exercise righteous dominion over their posterity throughout the Millennium. It almost seems impossible that mankind will be able to live together in peace for such an extended period of time. But with Satan bound and Christ as the chief lawgiver and judge over all, peace and contentment cannot help but permeate the entire world.

~ ~ ~

As difficult as it is to understand, while all men everywhere will be under the direction of the government of God, there will still be those during the early days of the Millennium who will not be members of the Church. We must not forget that those of a terrestrial order will also be a part of the Millennium and, for a time, may not choose to become Saints. These are good and honorable men and women who, by their works, merit a place in the millennial society. Yet, as time passes, more and more will be converted until whole nations will come up to the House of the Lord to serve him, for there will be but one god during the Millennium and one god only. All others will be done away with. There will be no more idols of stone or wood, nor any disposition whatsoever, to pay homage to spirit essences, or nature, or the dead, for all will worship the only true god, our Lord and Savior, Jesus Christ. Thus, missionary work will continue on into the Millennium until every knee bows and every tongue confesses adoration to the Lord, for the Millennium was designed to save souls, and for no other reason. No other church, sect or party of any kind can lead man to salvation, only Christ and his Church. Thus, all false doctrine will cease to be taught, all compulsory forms of governments will be done away with, and all people will come to worship at the feet of him who saves.

The Lord will teach the millennial man and woman the finer points of righteous living himself, much as he did in Jerusalem during his mortal ministry. He will teach from grassy knolls as well as in grand temples. He will sup with his people and visit their homes, and man will enjoy a personal and soul satisfying acquaintance with him.

> His voice shall again be heard on a mountain in Galilee as the Sermon on the Mount takes on a new and expanded meaning that none of us ever thought that it had. We shall hear again, in an upper room, as it were, the sermon on love and on the Second Comforter, and feel anew the power and spirit of the Intercessory Prayer. And to these will be added such other sermons as have never entered the heart of man as Jesus expounds the mysteries of eternity. Truly, truly did Isaiah promise, "From since the beginning of the world men have not heard, nor perceived by the ear, neither hath the eye seen, O God, beside thee, what he hath prepared for him that waiteth for him." (Isa. 64.4.)[9]

Because of man's willingness to work together for the common good and because of their enlightened state, the people in Zion, which by this time will encompass the entire world, will work together peacefully under the direction of the Savior and his servants in the priesthood. His greatest expectations are that man will become "one" as he and his father are "one." "That they all may be one; as thou, Father, art in me, and I in thee, that they also may be one in us" (John 17:21).

> The Savior sought continually to impress upon the minds of His disciples that a perfect oneness reigned among all celestial beings—That the Father and the Son and their Minister, the Holy Ghost, were one in their administration in Heaven and among the people pertaining to this earth. Between them and all the heavenly host there can be no disunion, no discord, no wavering on a manifestation; for such principle would differ widely from the character of Him who dictates them, who makes His throne the habitation of justice, mercy, equity, and truth. If the heavenly hosts are not one, they would be entirely unfit to dwell in the eternal burnings with the Father and Ruler of the Universe.[10]

Those who are at one with one another will not need the prison systems which were so necessary during past millenniums, for the laws of God will be obeyed without restraint. They will understand full well that the laws of God are just and created to elevate them, rather than just to keep them in line.

> The law and order of heaven are given expressly to increase celestial intelligence in the Saints, and to advance them in glory and power eternal. The man who walks uprightly before his God and infringes upon the rights of none, but feeds the hungry and clothes the naked, doing all he can to improve the condition of and happify his fellow-beings, walks above all law, and goes onward and still onward from conquering unto conquering. The laws of God are given to exalt the Saints to a higher state of glory—celestial felicity and powers, while the laws of men are too often made and enforced to subject the creature who disobeys them to increased depths of misery and degradation.

The law of God instills into the human souls a hatred of sin
by portraying the beauties and advantage of righteousness,
elevating it even above the desire to do wrong; the laws of
men, consisting chiefly in a code of penalties, against crime,
are made more to over-awe the creature than to instruct and
elevate the mind above the love of crime. Obedience to the
one brings the spirit of God—the Holy Ghost—to enlighten
and educate the mind with heavenly wisdom; obedience to
the other promises protection of life and property, but in
every instance leaves the mind still uninformed and in darkness. "The law of the Lord is perfect, converting the souls."
"Great peace have they who love Thy law."[11]

The kingdom of God will be a kingdom of laws and ordinances designed to exalt mankind. For such a system to function properly, however, the people themselves must freely and
intelligently sustain those in authority over them. This they
will do willingly, as has been the case in every dispensation
where the Church has been established among men.

The position we occupy is this: the Holy Ghost, which
has been given to all who have obeyed the gospel, and have
lived faithful to its precepts, takes of the things of God and
shows them forth through a living Priesthood to a people
enlightened and instructed and blessed by the Spirit of revelation from God, and the people thus enlightened, instructed
and blessed by the spirit of light, voluntarily and gladly sustain the Priesthood who minster unto them.[12]

By virtue of the holy priesthood, by love unfeigned, and
by a spirit of oneness the millennial man and woman will live
out their days in perfect unity. Such joy awaits them in this
state of congeniality that many pray for that glorious time to
come speedily. Yet the purposes of the Lord have not yet been
completed, there is still much to do. But, hopefully such glorious visions of that future time of peace will give us the added
strength we need to ward off the evil one and to prepare ourselves and the kingdom for the Lord's triumphant return.

~ ~ ~

Notes

1. Brigham Young, *Journal of Discourses,* 8:6–7.
2. Smith, *History of the Church,* 4:492–93.
3. Ibid, 5:64.
4. Pratt, *Key to the Science of Theology,* 71.
5. Brigham Young, *Journal of Discourses,* 6:342.
6. Ibid, 7:13.
7. Ibid, 2:170.
8. Ibid, 19:7.
9. McConkie, *Millennial Messiah,* 653.
10. Brigham Young, *Journal of Discourses,* 7:276.
11. Young, *Essential Brigham,* 166.
12. John Taylor, *Journal of Discourses,* 15:216.

Chapter Eight

The Millennial Society

The earth hath travailed and brought forth her strength; And truth is established in her bowels; And the heavens have smiled upon her; And she is clothed with the glory of her God; And he stands in the midst of his people. Glory, and honor, and power, and might be ascribed to our God; for he is full of mercy, Justice, grace, and truth, and peace, Forever and ever, Amen. (D&C 84:101–2)

The various societies of men will continue on into the Millennium and they will build cities of magnificent beauty and splendor. Families will live together much the same as they do today, and a social order will grow out of Zion that will fill up the whole earth.

> And that same sociality which exists among us here will exist among us there, only it will be coupled with eternal glory, which glory we do not now enjoy. (D&C 130:2)

The early beginnings of Zion, which will be organized in the New Jerusalem just prior to the Savior's Second Advent, will flourish during the Millennium and will spread across the land. The Holy Ghost will impart his gifts so liberally that man will be a new and noble creature and will so order his life that all individual actions will be for the common good. Charity will abound in this heavenly society and the people will be pure in heart. Thus, inhabitants of Zion will be one with God and with each other.

As the divine Spirit rains down upon the land and its inhabitants, knowledge will begin to flood the earth, including those mysteries which were hidden from the foundation of the world. Things both past, present and future, will be made known to the millennial man and woman and there will be nothing that will be withheld from their eyes. The knowledge of the world and of the entire universe will be laid out before them in all their splendor.

> The earth shall be full of the knowledge of the Lord as the waters cover the sea. Wherefore, the things of all nations shall be made known; yea, all things shall be made known unto the children of men. There is nothing which is secret save it shall be revealed; there is no work of darkness save it shall be made manifest in the light; and there is nothing which is sealed upon the earth save it shall be loosed. Therefore, all things which have been revealed unto the children of men shall at that day be revealed. (2 Ne. 30:15–18)

When the time is right, whether before or just after the Millennium is ushered in, the sealed portion of the Book of Mormon will be opened, and we will learn more about this earth, its creation, and man's ultimate mission and destiny. Other scriptures will also come forth, and we will be privileged to study the glorious manifestations that were given so liberally to prophets from all dispensations of time. And, as we grow in spirituality, we will learn to call down the powers of heaven and will learn more than we ever dreamed possible.

> If thou shalt ask, thou shalt receive revelation upon revelation, knowledge upon knowledge, that thou mayest know the mysteries and peaceable things—that which bringeth joy, that which bringeth life eternal. (D&C 42:61)

Although Zion will ultimately fill up the whole earth, its noble beginnings will be in Jackson County, Missouri, at a time when the world is filled with warring and contentions.

Once completed, that glorious city will continue to stand through the destruction of the last days and will become a beacon to the righteous who will seek refuge at her gates. When the Savior returns and the world as we know it comes to an end, Zion will be caught up in the clouds of heaven and will be joined with the City of Enoch, which was taken up so long ago. Then, when the cleansing is completed and the earth is prepared by sanctification to be inhabited again, they will descend together to exist upon the transfigured earth for a period of a thousand years. "Zion should again come on the earth, the city of Enoch which I have caught up unto myself" (JST Gen. 9:21). Prophets from all dispensations have prophesied about that glorious time and have longed to be a part of that great millennial society.

~ ~ ~

The plans for the building up of Zion were given to the Prophet Joseph Smith well over one hundred fifty years ago yet the Saints still wait patiently for the decree to commence that glorious building project. When that time finally arrives the Saints will commence that work with diligence that there might be a shelter from the coming storm and a place where the Son of God might rule and reign over his people during the glorious Sabbath of time. Every effort will be made to create a city of such magnificence that it will be a fit abode for the Savior and for those who abide his coming. Thus, there is much work yet to do and we must commence at a time when the ungodly are at our very doors. In speaking of that city, Brigham Young said:

> We will show them the most civil community—a community farther advanced in the arts of refinement than any other upon the earth. We will show them men and women the most profound in learning, and mechanics the most expert and ingenuous. We will show then men endowed with the most brilliant natural talent and the most wisdom that can be found in the world.[1]

John Taylor also elaborated on the glory of the Zion to come:

We believe that we shall rear splendid edifices, magnificent temples and beautiful cities that shall become the pride,
praise and glory of the whole earth. We believe that this people
will excel in literature, in science and the arts and in manu-
factures. In fact, there will be a concentration of wisdom, not
only of the combined wisdom of the world as it now exists,
but men will be inspired in regard to all these matters in a
manner and to an extent that they never have been before,
and we shall have eventually, when the Lord's purposes are
carried out, the most magnificent buildings, the most costly
clothing, and be the most healthy and the most intellectual
people that will reside upon the earth. This is part and par-
cel of our faith. . . . This is only a faint outline of some of
our views in relation to these things, and hence we talk
of returning to Jackson County to build the most magnificent temple that ever was formed on the earth and the most
splendid city that was ever erected; yea, cities, if you please.
The architectural designs of those splendid edifices, cities,
walls, gardens, bowers, streets, etc, will be under the direction of the Lord, who will control and manage all these matters; and the people, from the President down, will all be
under the guidance and direction of the Lord in all the pursuits of human life, until eventually they will be enabled to
erect cities that will be fit to be caught up—that when Zion
descends from above, Zion will also ascend from beneath,
and be prepared to associate with those from above. The
people will be so perfected and purified, ennobled, exalted,
and dignified in their feelings and so truly humble and most
worthy, virtuous and intelligent that they will be fit, when
caught up, to associate with that Zion that shall come down
from God out of heaven. This is the idea, in brief, that we
have entertained in relation to many of these things.[2]

Throughout all time, God has instructed his people to be
industrious and so it will be in Zion. There will be no idle or
slothful in that society and men will toil with their hands to
build their structures using the most skilled craftsmanship.
Moreover, the buildings they erect will far surpass in beauty

and design any our eyes have yet beheld. Magnificent gardens will surround them and majestic trees of every description will tower above and enhance the landscape.

Care will also be given to the beautification of homes and neighborhoods, and their gardens and orchards will spill over from yard to yard until the whole city is one continuous paradise. The cities of Zion will be laid out for the beauty, benefit, and care of all who live there, and men will enjoy a society of learning, growth, and enlightenment never dreamed of before.

After experiencing the operations of men during the first six thousand years of earth's existence, we can clearly see that only by using divine revelation can man hope to build a city that will be without the congestion, crime and the moral decay of our present time. Yet, with heavenly guidance we will create a city that will be for the good of all men collectively and which will bring them the greatest blessings of education, culture, and spiritual growth.

Joseph Smith was shown in vision the dimensions of such a city—a city which might have been built in his own day had the people been properly prepared. In General Conference on April 6th, 1837, Wilford Woodruff gave us this information regarding that occasion.

> He presented us in some degree with the plat of the city of Kirtland, which is the stronghold of the Daughter of Zion. The plan which he presented was given to him by vision, and the future will prove that the vision of Joseph concerning Jackson County, (Missouri), all the various stakes of Zion and of the redemption of Israel will be fulfilled in the time appointed of the Lord.[3]

While we have no way of knowing whether a new set of plans or perhaps a revision of the former will be given to harmonize with the advancement of time, according to those early instructions, the central city of Zion would be home to between fifteen thousand and twenty thousand people. The residential lots would be one half acre each, and would be set back twenty-five feet from the street leaving enough space in the front yard for small orchards or flower gardens. The yard in the back would also contain shrubs and trees and would be tailored to the individual needs of each builder. Gardens and an infinite variety of trees would predominate the landscape and create a lush paradise for each household within the confines of their own property. The streets would not run completely through in this arrangement. No two houses would face each other as one block of homes would face south while the next would run north. Thus, when looking from their windows the millennial family would enjoy the view of their neighbors gardens and fountains and their residence would become a peaceful retreat.

The early plans given to Joseph indicate the city of Zion will be square in dimension with three central plats of fifteen acres each. These three center plats will contain the Bishop's storehouse, administration buildings, and a grand temple with twenty-four compartments built in a circular form and arched over the center, one compartment for each of the priesthood quorums and one for the First Presidency. It will accommodate between twelve thousand and fifteen thousand people and will shine with heavenly light. It will be within the holy walls of this temple that the Savior himself will direct the affairs of his kingdom.

Surrounding the city will be land designated for agriculture, barns, stables, tabernacles and meetinghouses and parks and recreation. Farms in these surrounding plats will produce whatever food is necessary and each city will support itself. When the city is full, another city will be laid out in much the same manner until the world is filled up with a network of righteous communities.

Satellite cities in the New Jerusalem will be similar to the central stake but will have only one temple which will govern the affairs of that particular stake. The central stake, under the direction of the priesthood, will govern the entire kingdom. The Savior will preside as High Priest and rightful King. He will administer all the affairs of mankind in perfect order and in perfect righteousness.

As wonderful as that time will be, we should not expect the need to work will cease. The millennial man will work to build and sustain this glorious society and will find much joy in doing so. If gold or precious metals are used to adorn the temple walls, he will mine and refine it. If timber is to be used he will cut and mill it. Brick will be made and crops planted and harvested. Thus, the millennial man will be busily engaged in providing for his family and for the common needs of the community.

Schools of learning will also be available in that glorious society. Men and women alike will be trained to draw upon revelation for further light and knowledge, and both resurrected beings and angels will descend to teach and tutor them in the things of God. Thus, as we serve one another and gain further knowledge of God and of his handiwork, as we build and study and grow, we will more fully come to understand the purpose of life and will begin to experience that ultimate state of happiness called joy.

~ ~ ~

Those in the millennial society will also be united in all things pertaining to the kingdom. Temporally they will be equal in the distribution of wealth and possessions, and spiritually they will become a family of Saints who will love one another so much they will constantly be concerned about each others welfare. Because of the ennobling effects of such care, those who live during the Millennium will be as pure and delightsome a people as has ever lived upon the earth. Under these marvelous conditions men will have all things in common.

In keeping with this commonality, the affairs of the kingdom will be administered by the United Order which will allow for the growth and development of all within the union in their various capacities and circumstances.

Orson Pratt provides us with the reason for such an order.

An inequality in riches lays a foundation for pride, and many other evils. A family who are rich can build comfortable houses, purchase inheritances and fine carriages, clothe themselves in splendid attire, and educate their children in every branch of useful learning; while those who are poor labor and toil from morning until evening to procure a scanty subsidence; their families are coarsely clad, their children are not so highly educated. These opposite circumstances produce distinctions; the rich family do not feel to associate with the same degree of familiarity with the poor as they do with the rich: the sons and daughters of the rich seek for companions among those that are wealthy; the poor feel envious, because they are not rich. Besides the great inequalities in regard to the actual comforts of life, it produces great inequalities in education, in social circles, in marriage associations, and in almost every other respect. Hence, an inequality in property is the root and foundation of innumerable evils; it tends to division, and to keep asunder the social feelings that should exist among the people of God. It is the great barrier erected by the devil to prevent that unity and oneness which the Gospel requires; it is a principle originated in hell; it is the root of all evil.

Riches are not a curse, but they are a great blessing: it is inequality in riches that is a great curse. God has made all the riches of the earth, and the riches of all worlds, He made the gold, and the silver, and other precious metals. He formed the flocks and herds, and all useful animals: He has made the earth exceedingly rich; and He has given man dominion over all these things: The more His people enjoy of these things the better He is pleased; it is impossible for His people to become too rich: if the whole world, with all the treasures thereof, were in the hands of the saints, the Lord would still be delighted for them to have more. But these blessings have become a great curse to man, because they have been unequally possessed.[4]

Throughout all the ages of man there has been divisions between the rich and the poor with the rich often looking upon the poor with contempt. But in the Lord's plan of equity, the surplus in Zion would be used to elevate the poor so as to allow them to live in comfort and dignity. In the Doctrine and Covenants we learn how the Lord feels about that subject:

> That they may be equal in the bonds of heavenly things, yea, and earthly things also, for the obtaining of heavenly things.
>
> For if ye are not equal in earthly things ye cannot be equal in obtaining heavenly things;
>
> For if you will that I gave unto you a place in the Celestial World, you must prepare yourselves by doing the things which I have commanded you and required of you. (D&C 78:5–7)

What provisions did the Lord make in order to maintain this equality among His Saints permanently? He made this arrangement by law—that every man should be considered a steward.

> It is required of the Lord, at the hand of every steward, to render an account of his stewardship, both in time and in eternity.
>
> For he who is faithful and wise in time is counted worthy to inherit the mansions prepared for him of my Father. Verily I say unto you, the elders of the church in this part of my vineyard shall render an account of their stewardship unto the bishop, who shall be appointed of me in this part of my vineyard. These things shall be had on record, to be handed over unto the bishop in Zion. (D&C 72:3-6)

The surplus in Zion will be kept in the Bishop's storehouse and given to those who need it to fulfil their various stewardships. This surplus must be given freely and used by the common consent of the people.

> In your temporal things you shall be equal and this not grudgingly, otherwise the abundance of the manifestations of the Spirit shall be withheld.
>
> Now, this commandment I give unto my servants for their benefit while they remain, for a manifestation of my

blessings upon their heads, and for a reward of their diligence and for their security;

For food and for raiment; for an inheritance; for houses
and for lands, in whatsoever circumstances I, the Lord, shall
place them, and withersoever I, the Lord, shall send them.
(D&C 70:14–16)

In the Doctrine & Covenants we are instructed further
concerning the distribution of those things kept in the Bishop's
storehouse.

You are to be equal, or in other words, you are to have
equal claims on the properties (In the storehouse), for the
benefit of managing the concerns of your stewardships, every
man according to his wants and his needs, inasmuch as his
wants are just. (D&C 82:17)

There are numerous scriptures which tell us that God
wishes his sons and daughters to be happy. His ultimate desire
is that man might experience joy in all things. As we study
these scriptures we learn that it is the love of God that brings
us true joy. We further learn that it is obedience to his laws
which will bring us joy and God-like charity. It is service to
one's fellow man that will bring with it the only lasting happiness we can experience. Ultimately our happiness will be complete and never ending when we attain that exaltation which
will bring us into the presence of the Father and into a society
of celestial beings.

Love, then, is the grand key and describes that great force
which will unite mankind during the thousand years of millennial peace. Men will be so in tune to the needs of their
brethren and so quick to serve, that a binding of souls will take
place. Gentle persuasion and the most tender affections between
the Saints will create an atmosphere of the most charitable
feelings towards one another. Thus, in the Millennium every
man will esteem his neighbor as his brother and will deal with
him in friendship and love.

The Prophet Joseph Smith teaches us that:

Friendship is one of the grand fundamental principles of Mormonism; (it is designed) to revolutionize and civilize the world, and cause wars and contentions to cease and men to become friends and brothers. . . . It is a time honored adage that love begets love. Let us pour forth love—show forth our kindness unto all mankind, and the Lord will reward us with everlasting increase; cast our bread upon the waters and we shall receive it after many days, increased to a hundredfold. Friendship is like a blacksmith shop welding iron to iron; it unites the human family with its happy influence.[5]

Brigham Young asks:

How is it that the Latter-day Saints feel and understand alike, are of one heart and one mind, no matter where they may be when they receive the Gospel, whether in the north, or the south, the east, or the west, even to the uttermost parts of the earth? They receive that which was promised by the Savior when He was about to leave the earth, namely, the Comforter, that holy function from on high which recognizes one God, one faith, one baptism, whose mind is the will of God the Father, in whom there dwelleth unity of faith and action, and in whom there cannot be division or confusion; when they received this further light, it matters not whether they have seen each other or not, they have at once became brothers and sisters, having been adopted into the family of Christ through the bonds of the Everlasting Covenant, and all can then exclaim, in the beautiful language of Ruth, "Thy people shall be my people, and thy God my God!" And the fact that we receive this comforter, the Holy Ghost, is proof that the spirit, in warring with the flesh, has overcome, and by continuing in this state of victory over our sinful bodies we become the sons and daughters of God. Christ having made us free, and whosoever the Son makes free is free indeed. Having fought the good fight we then shall be prepared to lay our bodies down to rest to await the Morning of the Resurrection when they will come forth and be reunited with our spirits, the faithful, as it is said, receiving crowns, glory, immortality and eternal lives, even a fullness with the

Father, when Jesus shall present His work to the Father, saying, "Father here is the work thou gavest me to do." Then will they become Gods, even the sons of God; then will they become eternal fathers, eternal mothers, eternal sons and eternal daughters; being eternal in their organization they go from glory to glory, from power to power; they will never cease to increase and to multiply, worlds without end. When they receive their crowns, their dominions, they then will be prepared to frame earths like unto ours and to people them in the same manner as we have been brought forth by our parents, by our Father and God.[6]

~ ~ ~

In some of our modern, futuristic movies we see scenes of man's view of Utopia where men and women are portrayed as child-like in nature and giving obedience to some unseen entity. They laugh and play and neither sweat nor toil. They go on endlessly in much the same state of innocence, neither growing nor progressing in any way at all. How can joy be found in such a society? Where is the growth of individual talents and intellect? How can such a state of being produce true happiness or advancement of any kind? Only by service, work, and by developing charity towards all, can man find true happiness, and only by study and prayer can we come to know God and understand the gifts and glories that await us. God has placed a treasury of knowledge at our feet and only by grasping for it and growing in wisdom and in the pure love of Christ can we reach our fullest potential.

In the Book of Mormon we have a rich description of the Nephites who bound Satan by their righteousness and lived in harmony with one another for the space of two hundred years. These people were as mortal as any man or woman living today and were born with the same variety of dispositions, needs and weakness. In their mortal condition they struggled with a variety of appetites and the same insecurities that plague mankind today, but because of their righteous desire to do good, and because the Lord destroyed the wicked from among them, they were able to live worthy of the Spirit and to mingle together in peace for two hundred years.

In speaking of the Nephites who survived the destruction that accompanied the death of the Savior, Nephi says:

> And it came to pass that there was no contention in the land, because of the love of God which did dwell in the hearts of the people.
>
> And there were no envying, nor strife, nor tumults, nor whoredom, nor lyings, nor murders nor any manner of lasciviousness; and surely there was not a happier people among all the people who had been created by the hand of God. (4 Ne. 1:15–16)

If even in mortality men can experience happiness by obedience to the laws of God, how much better it will be in the Millennium when the powers of darkness are cast away and the Spirit of the Almighty rests constantly upon all the cities of Zion.

There must also be unity in Zion and a willingness for all men to work together for the common good. Because of the enlightening effects of the Spirit upon the mind and body the people of Zion will become pure in heart and will become one in purpose and will work together peacefully under the direction of the Savior and his servants in the priesthood.

A long held philosophy teaches that we learn to love those we serve. To be needed is a fundamental need of all mankind. By serving one another we meet not only our own instinctive needs, but we develop a bond for that person which in itself produces even more good fruit, for love begets love, service invites service. Compassion, kindness and charity all work together to create within us all the tender feelings that are necessary to strengthen, succor and sustain one another.

> Jesus offered up one of the most essential prayers that could possibly be offered up by a human or heavenly being— no matter who, pertaining to the salvation of the people, and

embodying a principle without which none can be saved, when he prayed the Father to make His disciples one, as He and His Father were one. He knew that if they did not become one, they could not be saved in the Celestial Kingdom of God. If persons do not see as He saw while in the flesh, hear as he heard, understand as he understood, and become precisely as he was, according to their several capacities and callings, they can never dwell with Him and His Father.[7]

~ ~ ~

The Millennium will not be a time of leisure or idleness, for there will be much work to do. There will be farming and merchandising. Homes and cities must be built, temples erected and temple work attended to. Fortunately, man will not weary of his work and responsibilities as the quickened man will no longer know the aches and pains of mortality or succumb to illness or disease. He will not be crippled or become depressed or mentally anguished, nor will he suffer the debilitating effects of old age. What wonderful things we could accomplish in this life if the handicaps of the flesh did not fetter us or keep us down. Nonetheless, this life is a time and place for learning and of being tested and tried. All of our experiences, whether good or bad, are for our ultimate benefit.

Those so blessed to be born during the Millennium will not have to pass through the portals of pain and despair, but regardless, they too must work out their salvation. They must grow step by step—gaining knowledge precept upon precept just as mortal man did. They must use their agency to do good works and must labor for their support and for that of their families. They must search for and find mates, marry within the holy temples and raise up righteous children to the Lord. They must worship and pray and search the scriptures for the meaning of life. They must learn to draw upon the powers of heaven and seek revelation from on high. They must help in the work of salvation for their kindred dead and must help in the work of reconciliation for the entire human family. All things must be in order. Families must be sealed, partners married, ordinances recorded in such a way that they coincide with the records of heaven. A great work must be done, a work that will take a millennium to complete and the millennial family must be the means of its completion. Those who live during the Sabbath of time will not be idle or pampered or living lives of perpetual luxury but will be united in love and purpose. They will work together to complete the work of sealing the entire human family together so that the Son can present the finished work to his Father when the time allotted is finished. There will be more work to do during the millennium than in all past dispensations combined. It will be a time of temple work, genealogy work, and of the reconciling of all things.

~ ~ ~

Notes

1. Brigham Young, *Journal of Discourses,* 8:10.

2. John Taylor, *Journal of Discourses,* 10:147.

3. Wilford Woodruff, *Conference Report,* April 6, 1837.

4. Pratt, *Equality and Oneness of the Saints,* 293–94, quoted in Andrus, *Doctrines of the Kingdom,* 272.

5. Smith, *History of the Church,* 1:517.

6. Brigham Young, *Journal of Discourses,* 18:259.

7. Ibid., 6:96.

Chapter Nine

The Work of Salvation

Let the earth break forth into singing. Let the
dead speak forth anthems of eternal praise to the King
Immanuel, who hath ordained, before the world was,
that which would enable us to redeem them out of their
prison; for the prisoners shall go free.(D&C 128:22)

There will be a great work to do for those who are privileged to live during the Millennium. With the earth at rest and Satan bound, the righteous will be anxiously engaged in the work of salvation for the entire human family. They will become saviors on Mount Zion, sealing husband to wife, father to son, mother to daughter, and family to family in the great Patriarchal Order. Thousands of temples will dot the globe during that Sabbath of time, and the spirit of God will pour down upon those holy structures in rich abundance and sanctify the work being done there.

Now, the ordinances of the temples are for the benefit and salvation of man and, thus, have eternal ramifications. And because the work must be done in the flesh, much rests upon the shoulders of man for its completion. Joseph Smith reveals the seriousness of neglecting this work.

The earth will be smitten with a curse unless there is a welding link of some kind or other between the fathers and the children upon some subject or other—and behold what is that subject? It is the baptism for the dead. For we without them cannot be made perfect; neither can they without us be made perfect. Neither can they nor we be made prefect without those who have died in the gospel also; for it is necessary in the ushering in of the dispensation of the fullness of times, which dispensation is now beginning to usher in, that a whole and complete and perfect union, and welding together of dispensations, and keys, and powers, and glories should take place, and be revealed from the days of Adam even to the present time. And not only this but those things which never have been revealed from the foundation of the world, but have been kept hid from the wise and prudent, shall be revealed unto babes and sucklings in this, the dispensation of the fullness of times. (D&C 128:18)

From the very beginning it was designed that families be linked together in a great family chain from Adam, the first of all men, down to the last man to live upon the earth before the earth and all her inhabitants are presented to the Father at the end of the Millennium. Parley P. Pratt explains that great Patriarchal Order, with Adam standing at the head of the celestial family.

> First, his most gracious and venerable majesty, King Adam, with his royal consort, Queen Eve, will appear at the head of the whole great family of the redeemed, and be crowned in their midst, as a king and a priest over them after the Order of the Son of God. . . . This venerable patriarch and sovereign will hold lawful jurisdiction over Abel, Noah, Enoch, Abraham, Isaac, Jacob, Joseph, Moses, the prophets apostles and saints of all ages and dispensations, who will all reverence and obey him as their venerable father and lawful sovereign. . . . They will then be organized each over his own department of government according to their birthright and office, in their families, generations and nations. . . . Each one will obey and be obeyed according to the connection which he sustains as member of the great celestial family.[1]

The everlasting link between families is of such importance that the entire Millennium will be devoted to the work of salvation. It will be of such importance that those on the other side of the veil will help the millennial man and woman fulfill their obligations to save their kindred dead and those who wait in the spirit world for their work to be done.

Brigham Young explains:

> The Gospel is now preached to the spirits in prison, and when the time comes for the servants of God to offici-ate for them, the names of those who have received the Gospel in the spirit will be revealed by the angels of God and the spirits of just men made perfect; also the places of their birth, the age in which they lived, and everything regarding them that is necessary to be recorded on earth, and they will then be saved so as to find admittance into the presence of God, with their relatives who have officiated for them.[2]

He explains further that because the research needed to link families together will be difficult, since so many of Father's children lived out their days and then died without leaving records behind, help will come from the world of spirits.

> When his Kingdom is established upon the earth, and Zion built up, the Lord will send his servants as saviors upon Mount Zion. The servants of God who have lived on earth in ages past will reveal where different persons have lived who have died without the Gospel, give their names, and say "now go forth, ye servants of God, and exercise your rights and privileges; go and perform the ordinances of the house of God for those who have passed their probation without the Gospel, and for all who will receive any kind of salvation; bring them up to inherit the celestial, terrestrial, and telestial kingdoms," and probably many other king-doms not mentioned in the scriptures; for every person will receive according to his capacity and according to the deeds done in the body, whether good or bad, much or little.[3]

There were periods of time during earth's long history when the gospel was not readily available to the masses of the world. There were also times when the gospel was taken away

113

because of wickedness. Thus, millions have lived and died without the opportunity to hear and embrace the gospel and partake of its saving ordinances. However, by divine decree, those who were honorable among them, those who would have accepted it had they had the opportunity while in the flesh, will be taught in the spirit world and will be given the same advantage as those who embraced it while in mortality. We gain a measure of understanding on the matter from a vision given Joseph F. Smith.

> And thus was the gospel preached to the dead. And the chosen messengers went forth to declare the acceptable day of the Lord, and proclaim liberty to the captives who were bound; even unto all who would repent of their sins and receive the gospel. Thus was the gospel preached to those who had died in their sins, without a knowledge of the truth, or in transgression, having rejected the prophets. These were taught faith in God, repentance from sin, vicarious baptism for the remission of sins, the gift of the Holy Ghost by the laying on of hands, and all other principles of the gospel that were necessary for them to know in order to qualify themselves that they might be judged according to men in the flesh, but live according to God in the spirit.[4]

Now, the work performed by proxy for the dead in no way assures the departed a glorious resurrection. They, too, must accept or reject the gospel and its saving ordinances by the exercise of their agency just as all men must. But because men's dispositions do not change from one sphere to another, those inclined to reject the gospel in mortality will most likely reject it in the world of spirits as well. Likewise, those who would have accepted it in this life, had they had the opportunity, will undoubtedly accept it in the next life also. But, as is always the case with new converts, those who do so, must sink beneath the water and come up a new man or woman, reborn and cleansed from all iniquity. The ordinance of baptism is an earthly ordinance, however, and cannot be performed in the spirit.

> It is well understood that the ordinances of the Gospel, such as baptism and the laying on of hands, pertain to this life, therefore, those who have died without the Gospel, cannot act in their own behalf. Someone in mortal life must act for them. Neither can those who have received the resurrection officiate and stand for themselves, for they too, belong to another life.[5]

It is no wonder the great bulk of this work will be performed during the Millennium. Only when help is freely given from the other side of the veil can so great a work be accomplished. The hearts of men will truly be turned toward their fathers during the Millennium, and a steady stream of worthy saints will enter the temples to further the work.

> If we preserve ourselves in the truth and live so that we shall be worthy of the Celestial Kingdom, by and by we can officiate for those who have died without the Gospel— the honest, honorable, truthful and virtuous and pure. By and by it will be said unto us, Go ye forth and be baptized for them and receive the ordinances for them, and the hearts of the children will be turned to the fathers who have slept in their graves and they will secure to them eternal life. This must be, lest the Lord come and smite the earth with a curse. The children of God will go forth and revive this law for those who have slept for thousands of years who died without the Gospel. Jesus will prepare a way to bring them up into his presence. But were it not for the few who will be prepared here on the earth to officiate when the Lord shall come to reign King of nations, what would be the condition of the world? They would sleep and sleep on; but the way is prepared for their redemption.[6]

A staggering amount of work awaits the millennial man and woman. Once again Brigham Young assures us that help will be available:

> When we have the privilege of building up Zion, the time will come for saviors to come up on Mount Zion. Some of those who are not in mortality will come along and say, "Here are a thousand names I wish you to attend to in

this temple, and when you have got through with them I
will give you another thousand;" and the Elders of Israel
and their wives will go forth to officiate for their forefathers, the men for the men and the women for the women.[7]

Oh, what a glorious time for those who wait on the other
side; those who, after hearing the gospel in the world of spirits and accepted it, or those who had already accepted it in
morality but died before receiving their ordinances, will shout
for joy when their work is finally performed for them.

~ ~ ~

The keys of the sealing power and the higher ordinances
of the temple were restored to Joseph Smith and Oliver Cow-
dery on April 3, 1836, in the Kirtland Temple. After several
wondrous visions burst forth upon Joseph and Oliver, the
ancient Prophet Elijah appeared to them and said:

Behold, the time has fully come, which was spoken
by the mouth of Malachi—testifying that he (Elijah) should
be sent, before the great and dreadful day of the Lord come—

To turn the hearts of the fathers to the children, and
the children to the fathers, lest the whole earth be smitten
with a curse—

Therefore, the keys of this dispensation are commit-
ted into your hands; and by this ye may know that the great
and dreadful day of the Lord is near, even at the doors.
(D&C 110:14–16)

Thus, a great work is before us, a work which has begun
in our day, but will need a millennium to complete.

~ ~ ~

Happily, the tender love of husbands and wives will also
continue on into eternity for those who were united by the
everlasting covenants of marriage in the temple. This sealing
is the crowning jewel of all the sacred ordinances and with it
comes all the promised blessings of eternity. It is within the

holy union that children are sealed to their parents and secured a place in the family of God throughout all time and eternity. There is no greater blessing that we can aspire to, for with compliance to those sacred covenants come the blessings of exaltation. The family unit is designed to continue on forever. Thus, as family is sealed to family and generation to generation, the divine Patriarchal Order will grow until all the worthy families of the earth are united and sealed and can then be presented to the Father.

Parley P. Pratt learned of the principle of temple marriage at the feet of the Prophet Joseph Smith.

> During these interviews he taught me many great and glorious principles concerning God and the heavenly order of eternity. It was at this time that I received from him the first idea of eternal family organization, and the eternal union of the sexes in those inexpressibly endearing relationship which none but the highly intellectual, the refined and pure in heart, know how to prize, and which are at the very foundation of everything worthy to be called happiness.
>
> Till then I had learned to esteem kindred affections and sympathies as appertaining solely to this transitory state, as something from which the heart must be entirely weaned, in order to be fitted for its heavenly state.
>
> It was Joseph Smith who taught me how to prize the endearing relationships of father and mother, husband and wife, of brother and sister, son and daughter.
>
> It was from him that I learned that the wife of my bosom might be secured to me for time and all eternity; and the refined sympathies and affection which endeared us to each other emanated from the foundation of divine eternal love. It was from him that I learned that we might cultivate these affections, and grow and increase in same to all eternity; while the result of our endless union would be an offspring as numerous as the stars of heaven or the sands of the sea shore.
>
> It was from him that I learned the true dignity and destiny of a son of God, clothed with an eternal priesthood,

as the patriarch and sovereign of his countless offspring. It was from him that I learned that the highest dignity of womanhood was, to stand as a queen and priestess to her husband, and to reign for ever and ever as the queen mother of her numerous and still increasing offspring.

I had loved before, but I knew not why. But now I loved—with a pureness—and intensity of elevated, exalted feeling, which would lift my soul from the transitory things of this grovelling sphere and expand it as the ocean. I felt that God was my heavenly Father indeed; that Jesus was my brother and that the wife of my bosom was an immortal eternal companion; a kind ministering angel, given to me as a comfort, and a crown of glory for ever and ever, In short, I could now love with the spirit and with the understanding also.

Yet, at that time, my dearly beloved brother, Joseph Smith, had barely touched a single key; had merely lifted a corner of the veil and given me a single glance into eternity.[8]

In speaking of the sealing ordinances of the temple the Prophet teaches us:

These additional powers, included all the keys that belong to the holy priesthood on the earth, or were ever revealed to man in any dispensation, and which admit men and women within the veil. They enable them to pass by the angels and the Gods, until they get into the presence of the Father and the Son. They make of them kings and priests, queens and priestesses to God, to rule and reign as such over their posterity and those who may be given to them by adoption. . . . It gives them the right to the tree of life, and the "seal of the living God in their foreheads," spoken of by John the revelator. No marvel, then, that the Lord requires sacred places for such great and glorious things.[9]

~ ~ ~

The white robes of purity will hang in every closet as worthy men and women make the work of salvation their highest priority.

The mission of our elder brother, Jesus Christ, must continue on until the entire human race has been accounted for, and until the work for those who would accept the gospel has been completed.

Jesus had not finished His work when His body was slain, neither did He finish it after His resurrection from the dead; although He had accomplished the purpose for which he then came to the earth, He had not fulfilled all His work. And when will He? Not until He has redeemed and saved every son and daughter of our father, Adam, that have ever been or will ever be upon this earth to the end of time, except the sons of Perdition. That is His mission. We will not finish our work until we have saved ourselves, and then not until we shall have saved all depending upon us; for we are to become saviors upon Mount Zion as well as Christ. We are called to this mission. The dead are not perfect without us, neither are we without them. We have a mission to perform for and in their behalf; we have a certain work to do in order to liberate those who because of their ignorance and unfavorable circumstances in which they were placed while here, are unprepared for eternal life; we have to open the door for them, by performing ordinances which they cannot perform for themselves, and which are essential to their release from the "prison house," to come forth and live according to God in the spirit, and be judged according to men in the flesh.[10]

We are instructed further regarding those who wait on the other side for their ordinances to be performed.

They have passed the ordeals, and are beyond the possibility of personally officiating for the remission of their sins and for their exaltation, consequently they are under the necessity of trusting in their friends, their children and their children's children to officiate for them that they may be brought up into the Celestial Kingdom of God.[11]

Brigham Young asks a sobering question.

What do you suppose the fathers would say if they could speak from the dead? Would they not say, "we have lain here thousands of years, here in this prison house, waiting for this dispensation to come? Here we are, bound and fettered, in the association of those who are filthy?" What would they whisper in our ears? Why if they had the power the very thunders of heaven would be in our ears, if we could but realize the importance of the work we are engaged in. All the angels in heaven are looking at this little handful of people, and stimulating them to the salvation of the human family. So also are the devils in hell looking at this people, too, and trying to overthrow us, and the people are still shaking hands with the servants of the devil, instead of sanctifying themselves and calling upon the Lord and doing the work which he has commanded us and put into our hands to do. When I think upon this subject, I want the tongues of seven thunders to wake up the people.[12]

The great work of salvation will come at a time when Jesus Christ will dwell among his people personally and will reveal the mysteries of eternity to them.

And to them will I reveal all mysteries, yea all the hidden mysteries of my kingdom from days of old, and for ages to come, will I make known unto them the good pleasure of my will concerning all things pertaining to my kingdom.

Yea, even the wonders of eternity shall they know, and things to come will I show them, even the things of many generations.

And their wisdom shall be great, and their understanding reach to heaven; and before them the wisdom of the wise shall perish and the understanding of the prudent shall come to naught.

For by my Spirit will I enlighten them, and by my power will I make known unto them the secrets of my will—yea, even those things which eye has not seen, nor ear heard, nor yet entered into the heart of man. (D&C 76:7–10)

With knowledge of this nature given freely to the righteous, the work of salvation can go forth in a way never dreamed of before, and our love for our forefathers will overpower us until their temple work is completed. Tears of love will undoubtedly flow freely from both sides of the veil.

The shining spires of the temples will dot the globe during the Millennium, and the peaceful landscaped grandeur of the temple settings will draw us away from our daily endeavors and into those sacred halls. There we will mingle with the most devoted and honorable Saints who have ever lived upon the earth. We will form friendships and have warm communion with one another. That sacred setting will foster love between not only earthly Saints, but also for those who wait beyond the veil. What a glorious experience it will be. Never will man be happier than when he is attending to the salvation of the human family; the eternal family of God, our Father, who waits patiently for our return.

~ ~ ~

Notes

1. McKinlay, *Life Eternal*, 197.
2. Brigham Young, *Journal of Discourses,* 9:317.
3. Ibid., 6:347.
4. McKinlay, *Life Eternal,* 197.
5. Joseph F. Smith. "The Way to Perfection," 325.
6. Brigham Young, *Journal of Discourses*, 14,. 148.
7. McKinley, *Life Eternal*, 237.
8. Pratt, *Autobiography,* 297–98.
9. Smith, *Juvenile Instructor* 15 (May 1, 1880): 111
10. Smith, *Gospel Doctrine,* 442.
11. Brigham Young, *Journal of Discourses,* 18:238.
12. Ibid., 18:304.

Chapter Ten

Judgment and Glory

*And it shall come to pass that when all men shall
have passed from this first death unto life, insomuch
as they have become immortal, they must appear
before the judgment . . . and then must they be judged
according to the holy judgment of God. (2 Ne. 9:15)*

The ultimate goal of every man or woman born into mortality should be to be saved in the Celestial Kingdom of God. Yet for many that seems like an impossible dream. While it is true that our journey through mortality is often discouraging, due to Satan's constant buffetings, the Father has provided lights along the way and has prepared every advantage possible that each of his children might attain that final reward.

Not only did he prepare a world for them, that they might gain new experiences and develop mastery over self, but he also provided them with bodies of flesh and blood, which when glorified and in their resurrected state, would bring them unspeakable joy. He gave them prophets to act as his mouthpiece during their sojourn on earth and scriptures to be their guide. As a final gesture of his love, he prepared a Savior for them and marked the path that all might find their way home. Throughout the long history of the world the great Elohim has done all that he could to lead and guide his children through the dark mists of mortality and back into his presence. Moreover, in a horrific effort to preserve the righteous he cleansed the earth of wickedness not just once during the days of Noah, but will do so again at the Second Advent of his Only Begotten Son who will destroy the wicked, imprison Lucifer, and usher in the long awaited Millennium.

There will come a time near the end of the Millennium when the hearts of many will turn cold again, just as in times of old. They will forsake their covenants and leave the United Order. They will be lifted up in pride again and deny the power of God (D&C 29:22). Thus, Lucifer will be let loose from his chains to try and tempt away as many of God's children as he can. More than that, he will be arrogant enough to think he can still win the war. Thus, as the Millennium draws to a close, he will "gather together his armies," one last time to battle against the Saints (D&C 88:111). Consequently, the winding up scene of the earth's terrestrial condition will be much as it was before the final days of its telestial state. Just as the forces of evil will join togther in a great battle at Armageddon prior to the Savior's Second Coming, so will the forces of evil band together at the end of the Millennium. But, Lucifer will only "reign for a little season, and then cometh the end of the earth." (D&C 43:31.)

Michael, the archangel, will lead the Lord's army during that terrible time, just as he always has.

> And Michael, the seventh angel, even the archangel, shall gather together his armies, even the hosts of heaven.
>
> And the devil shall gather together his armies; even the hosts of hell, and shall come up to battle against Michael and his armies. . . . For Michael shall fight their battles, and shall overcome him who seeketh the throne of him who sitteth upon the throne, even the Lamb. (D&C 88:112-113, 115)

Once again, fire from heaven will end the conflict just as it will at the end of the earth's telestial state.

> And they went up on the breadth of the earth, and compassed the camp of the saints about, and the beloved city: and

fire came down from God out of heaven, and devoured them.

And the devil that deceived them was cast into the lake of fire and brimstone, where the beast and the false prophet are, and shall be tormented day and night for ever and ever. (Rev. 20:9–10)

Thus, the long reign of Lucifer will finally be over and he and his devilish angels will be cast out, but this time for good.

And the devil and his armies shall be cast away into their own place, that they shall not have power over the saints any more at all. (D&C 88:114)

Now, just as the earth endured great changes at the time of the Second Coming and the ushering in of the Millennium, so will the earth endure great changes at the end of the Millennium. This time, however, she will be adorned with celestial glory for which purpose she was created in the first place.

And the end shall come, and the heaven and the earth shall be consumed and pass away, and there shall be a new heaven and a new earth.

For all old things shall pass away, and all things shall become new, even the heaven and the earth, and all the fulness thereof, both men and beasts, the fowls of the air, and the fishes of the sea;

And not one hair, neither mote, shall be lost, for it is the workmanship of mine hand. (D&C 29:23-25)

Mother Earth will thus become a celestial orb—designed for the eternal habitat of all those who merit the presence of the Father and the Son.

Therefore, it must needs be sanctified from all unrighteousness that it may be prepared for the celestial glory;

For after it hath filled the measure of its creation, it shall be crowned with glory, even with the presence of God the Father:

That bodies who are of the Celestial Kingdom may possess it forever and ever; for, for this intent was it made and created, and for this intent are they sanctified. (D&C 88:18–20)

For this intent was it created! Once more we receive affirmation that the plan of our Father is a plan for *our* exaltation, for *our* glory and for *our* happiness. By divine decree, a place of glory is being prepared for us that will out-shine the sun and will be the home of the faithful forever and ever.

Before the earth passes away, however, all mankind must be judged—the most dreaded and most anticipated event to take place since the world began.

> But, behold, verily I say unto you, before the earth shall pass away, Michael, mine archangel, shall sound his trump, and then shall all the dead awake, for their graves shall be opened, and they shall come forth—yea, even all.
>
> And the righteous shall be gathered on my right hand unto eternal life; and the wicked on my left hand will I be ashamed to own before the Father;
>
> Wherefore I will say unto them—Depart from me, ye cursed, into everlasting fire, prepared for the devil and his angels. (D&C 29:26–28)

It will be both a great and terrible day. It will not only include those who were resurrected when the Savior returned in all his glory to usher in his millennial reign, but it will also include those who were assigned to come forth at the end of the Millennium after the price had been paid.

> Therefore the wicked remain as though there had been no redemption made, except it be the loosing of the bands of death; for behold, the day cometh that all shall rise from the dead and stand before God, and be judged according to their works. (Alma 11:41)

Just a trace of information has been given concerning the fate of Lucifer and the sons of perdition, those who were given sure knowledge of Christ and then denied him.

> (Jesus)—Who glorified the Father, and saves all the works of his hands, except those sons of perdition who deny

the Son after the Father has revealed him.

Wherefore, he saves all except them—they shall go away into everlasting punishment, which is endless punishment, which is eternal punishment, to reign with the devil and his angels in eternity, where their worm dieth not, and the fire is not quenched, which is their torment—

And the end thereof, neither the place thereof, nor their torment, no man knows;

Neither was it revealed, neither is, neither will be revealed unto man, except to them who are made partakers thereof;

Nevertheless, I the Lord, show it by vision unto many, but straightway shut it up again;

Wherefore, the end, the width, the height, the depth, and the misery thereof, they understand not, neither any man except those who are ordained unto this condemnation. (D&C 76:43–49)

~ ~ ~

The time will come when every soul who ever lived will stand before the bar of justice and be given their just rewards. It will be a day when the works of righteousness will be heralded from the house tops and their ultimate rewards meted out, but also a day when the wicked will be reap the rewards of a life of sin. Thus, it will be a day when men will be rewarded according to their works, whether good or bad, little or much.

Yea, and blessed are the dead that die in the Lord, from henceforth, when the Lord shall come, and old things shall pass away, and all things become new, they shall rise from the dead and shall not die after, and shall receive an inheritance before the Lord, in his holy city. (D&C 63:49)

Of all the events to transpire among men, the judgment is the most feared. Even in our childhood we shrank from punishment or cringed with guilt when we failed to be obedient to the strict commands of our parents or teachers. As time passed, we became aware of the laws of the land and learned that we must also obey those laws. As more time passed we became aware of our Creator and came to understand there was an even greater law than man's—that of God's. And, once again, we were put under the strict command of obedience. As our understanding grew, we came to understand Heavenly Father's great love for us and that blessings awaited those who obeyed his commands. Likewise, we learned that divine punishment fell upon those who disobeyed. Thus, our love and respect for deity was soon coupled with godly fear lest we, too, offend the Lord, God Omnipotent.

From the very beginning, the Father imparted a gift to his children—that of agency. By this great gift we could become individuals who acted and were acted upon by the forces of both good and evil. At the time of our births another gift was given—the light of Christ, to act as our conscience and whisper correct principles in our ears, much as the tiny cricket did for the wooden puppet in the children's story, Pinocchio. The light of Christ will not leave us, however, or get lost or become ill and die. It will remain with us throughout our lives, that we be not overcome by the promptings of the devil. The powerful influence of the Holy Ghost provides even further light and knowledge to those properly baptized. Thus, we have not been left alone in this dark and dreary world. Moreover, prayer provides a constant conduit between God and his children allowing for further strength, comfort, and instruction.

Such gifts were given that all mankind might discern right from wrong, and, thus, by the age of accountability, decide for themselves whether to choose good or evil. Yet, because of our lack of experience, for which purpose we came to earth, or because of our upbringing or weakness of the flesh, sometimes we fall victim to sin. Our only recourse then is repentance and a cleansing of our souls, for no unclean thing can enter into the bosom of the Father. Thus, for those who fall by the wayside and succumb to sin, the road seems bleak indeed. A heart racked with sorrow and guilt becomes our hell and Satan would have us believe there is no hope. But we must never lose sight of the fact that God sacrificed his Only Begotten Son for such souls, for those who lose their way, the only requirement being a penitent heart and proper repentance. The Savior's love will reach into hell itself to pluck up the souls of the truly repentant, and, by his ransom, save them in whichever kingdom they merit by their works. There is no doubt that in the day of judgement a myriad of those who are recipients of that great gift will kneel before our elder brother Jesus, and, with tears in their eyes, give thanks for his sacrifice in their behalf.

The judgment will take into consideration all the conditions men or woman were faced with in mortality; their sufferings and trials, their growth or lack of it, their humanity to their fellow men or their selfishness and baser actions. They will be judged by the intent of their hearts and by the light and knowledge given in their day and age. Thus, all men will be judged fairly and honesty and will be placed in a degree of glory merited by their own actions.

The Lord, Jesus, himself will judge his people.

> And I saw a great white throne, and him that sat on it, from whose face the earth and the heaven fled away; and there was found no place for them.
>
> And I saw the dead, small and great stand before God; and the books were opened; and another book was opened, which is the book of life; and the dead were judged out of those things which were written in the books, according to their works,
>
> And the sea gave up the dead which were in it; and death and hell delivered up the dead which were in them: and they were judged, every man, according to their works.
>
> And death and hell were cast into the lake of fire. This is the second death.
>
> And whosoever was not found written in the book of life was cast into the lake of fire. (Rev. 20:11–15)

129

Wicked men will have a perfect recollection of all their uncleanness while those who lived lives of honor will recall their righteousness and will be clothed upon with the robes of purity.

> And then cometh the judgment of the Holy One upon them; and then cometh the time that he that is filthy shall be filthy still; and he that is righteous shall be righteous still; he that is happy shall be happy still; and he that is unhappy shall be unhappy still. (Morm. 9:14)

After the judgment, men will be assigned to their everlasting rewards. Their works will have judged them; the books will have judged them; the Savior will have judged them, and now they must be given the ultimate rewards of their actions and assigned to whichever glory they've earned by their works.

~ ~ ~

Many mansions have been prepared for the family of God; mansions of such glory that even the lesser kingdom will far surpass our greatest expectations. Even those who merit a terrestrial or a telestial kingdom will be comfortable and happy in their surroundings. Men will be assigned those kingdoms that best fit their desires and capacities. They will be assigned by the merit of their works and will be given an eternal inheritance which will bring them the greatest measure of happiness.

> These words set forth the fact to which Jesus referred when he said, "In my Father's house are many mansions." How many I am not prepared to say; but here are three distinctly spoken of: the celestial, the highest; the terrestrial, the next below it, and the telestial, the third. If we were to take the pains to read what the Lord has said to his people in the latter days we should find that he has made provision for all the inhabitants of the earth; every creature who desires, and who strives in the least, to overcome evil and subdue iniquity within himself or herself, and to live worthy of a glory, will possess one. We who have received the fullness of the Gospel of the Son of God, or the Kingdom of heaven

that has come to earth, are in possession of those laws, ordinances, commandments and revelations that will prepare us, by strict obedience, to inherit the Celestial Kingdom, to go into the presence of the Father and the Son.[1]

Joseph Smith was shown in vision the magnificence of three degrees of glory.

And thus we saw, in the heavenly vision, the glory of the telestial, which surpasses all understanding;

And thus we saw the glory of the terrestrial which excels in all things the glory of the telestial, even in glory, and in power, and in might, and in dominion.

And thus we saw the glory of the celestial, which excels in all things—where God, even the Father reigns upon his throne forever and ever; (D&C 76:89, 91-92)

Of those who inherit the higher kingdom we are told:

They are they who received the testimony of Jesus, and believed on his name and were baptized after the manner of his burial, being buried in the water in his name and this according to the commandment which he has given—

That by keeping the commandments they might be washed and cleansed from all their sins, and receive the Holy Spirit by the laying on of the hands of him who is ordained and sealed unto this power;

And who overcome by faith, and are sealed by the Holy Spirit of promise, which the Father sheds forth upon all those who are just and true. (D&C 76:51-53)

Of the terrestrial order we learn:

And again, we saw the terrestrial world, and behold and lo, these are they who are of the terrestrial, whose glory differs from that of the church of the Firstborn who have received the fulness of the Father, even as that of the moon differs from the sun in the firmament.

Behold, these are they who died without law;

And also they who are the spirits of men kept in prison, whom the Son visited, that they might be judged according to men in the flesh;

131

Who received not the testimony of Jesus in the flesh, but afterwards received it.

These are they who are honorable men of the earth, who were blinded by the craftiness of men,

These are they who receive of the presence of the Son, but not of the fulness of the Father. (D&C 76:71–75, 77)

Of the lesser kingdom we learn the following:

And again, we saw the glory of the telestial, which glory is that of the lesser, even as the glory of the stars differs from that of the glory of the moon in the firmament.

These are they who receive not the gospel of Christ, neither the testimony of Jesus.

These are they who deny not the Holy Spirit.

These are they who are thrust down to hell.

These are they who shall not be redeemed from the devil unit the last resurrection, until the Lord, even Jesus Christ the Lamb, shall have finished his work. (D&C 76:81–85)

Brigham Young teaches us:

How many kingdoms there are has not been told to us; they are innumerable. The disciples of Jesus were to dwell with him. Where will the rest go? Into kingdoms prepared for them, where they will live and endure. Jesus will bring forth, by his own redemption, every son and daughter of Adam, except the sons of perdition, who will be cast into hell. Others will suffer the wrath of God—will suffer all the Lord can demand at their hands, or justice can require of them; and when they have suffered the wrath of God till the utmost farthing is paid, they will be brought out of prison. Is this dangerous doctrine to preach? Some consider it dangerous; but it is true that every person who does not sin away the day of grace, and become an angel to the Devil, will be brought forth to inherit a kingdom of glory.[2]

He continues:

So far as mortality is concerned, millions of the

inhabitants of the earth live according to the best light they have—according to the best knowledge they possess. I have told you frequently that they will receive according to their works; and all, who live according to the best principles in their possession, or that they can understand, will receive peace, glory, comfort, joy and a crown that will be far beyond what they are anticipating. They will not be lost.[3]

The work of salvation has been a heavy burden for the Son. He has been carrying his load from before the world was created, but now the work is completed and he can present it to the Father.

> But, behold, the righteous, the saints of the Holy One of Israel, they who have believed in the Holy One of Israel, they who have endured the crosses of the world, and despised the shame of it, they shall inherit the kingdom of God, which was prepared for them from the foundation of the world, and their joy shall be full forever. (2 Ne. 9:18)

~ ~ ~

Notes

1. Brigham Young, *Journal of Discourses,* 14:148.
2. Ibid., 8:154.
3. Ibid., 6:332.

Chapter Eleven

Celestial Burnings

*To him that overcometh will I grant to sit with me
in my throne, even as I also overcame, and am set
down with my Father in his throne. (Rev.3:21)*

It is finished! Mankind has been tested and tried, the family of God has been joined together in the great Patriarchal Order, and men have been judged according to their works and assigned their everlasting inheritance. The Son can now present the work to his Father and receive his own reward. Brigham Young teaches us:

> Our spirits, thousands of years ago, were first begotten; and at the consummation of all things, when the Savior has finished his work and presented it to the Father, he will be crowned. None of you will receive your crowns of glory, immortality, and eternal lives before he receives his. He will be crowned first, and then we shall be crowned, every one in his order; for the work is finished, and the spirit is complete in its organization with the tabernacle. The world is the first to be redeemed, and the people last to be crowned upon it.[1]

In the Doctrine and Covenants we read:

> Christ shall have subdued all enemies under his feet, and shall have perfected his work;
>
> When he shall deliver up the Kingdom, and present it unto the Father spotless, saying: I have overcome and have

trodden the wine-press alone, even the wine-press of the fierceness of the wrath of Almighty God.

Then shall he be crowned with the crown of his glory, to sit on the throne of his power to reign forever and ever. (D&C 76:106–108)

The great God, Elohim, has been preparing for this day since before the foundation of the earth was laid—the day his children would finally come home. While there are those who wonder just how many of God's children will actually make it back into his presence, considering the struggles of mortality, rest assured that untold millions will find their way back and be saved in the highest degree of heaven.

Sin is rampant around us, and always seems to have been so, thus it is often difficult to see the outcome of man's probationary state. But, if we expand our vision to include all those who will live during the peaceful millennial years, we will be able to see that billions of God's children will live out there lives and pass on to the other side in glory. Especially if we include those billions who will go on to exaltation because of the work performed for them vicariously while they waited in the world of spirits.

> Hundreds of millions of human beings have been born, lived out their short earthly span, and passed away, ignorant alike of themselves and of the plan of salvation provided for them. It gives great consolation, however, to know that this glorious plan devised by Heaven follows them into the next existence, offering for their acceptance eternal life and exaltation to thrones, dominions, principalities, and powers in the presence of their Father and God, through Jesus Christ.[2]

The Father's plan for the salvation of his children is a good one, and innumerable hosts of men and women will be saved. When death as we know it ceases and war and disease are a thing of the past, it is conceivable that more people will be born during the Millennium than in all ages past.

In speaking of the blessings promised to the seed of Abraham, the Lord says this:

> And as touching Abraham and his seed, out of the world they should continue; both in the world and out of the world should they continue as innumerable as the stars; or, if ye were to count the sands upon the seashore ye could not number them. (D&C 132:30)

Those chosen by the merits of their works to be born during the Millennium will grow up without sin unto salvation. Thus, untold millions will be born and will live worthy of exaltation. Consider further, the children from all past ages who were born and then died before the age of accountability. Consider the righteous souls who lived in the cities of Enoch and Salem and those who enjoyed a righteous society during the Nephite era; all will be given a celestial reward. The Father's work and his glory is to save souls and great hosts of the righteous will enjoy exaltation. But, with the closing of the Millennium the time has come to prepare the earth for their inheritance—a celestial orb to dwell upon.

> This world, so benighted at present, and so lightly esteemed by infidels, when it becomes celestialized, it will be like the sun and be prepared for the inhabitation of the Saints, and be brought back into the presence of the Father and the Son. It will not then be an opaque body as it now is, but it will be like the stars of the firmament, full of light and glory; it will be a body of light. John compared it, in its celestialized state, to a sea of glass.[3]

Joseph Smith gives us further instruction about the condition of the celestialized earth in section 130 of the Doctrine and Covenants:

> The angels do not reside on a planet like this earth;
> But they reside in the presence of God, on a globe like a sea of glass and fire, where all things for their glory are manifest, past, present, and future, and are continually before the Lord.

> The place where God resides is a great Urim and Thummim.
>
> This earth, in its sanctified and immortal state, will be made like unto crystal and will be a Urim and Thumim to the inhabitants who dwell thereon, whereby all things pertaining to an inferior kingdom, or all kingdoms of a lower order, will be manifest to those who dwell upon it; and this earth will be Christ's. (D&C 130:6–9)

We learn in the Doctrine and Covenants that there are three degrees in the Celestial Kingdom.

> In the celestial glory there are three heavens or degrees;
>
> And in order to obtain the highest, a man must enter into this order of the priesthood [meaning the new and everlasting covenant of marriage];
>
> And if he does not, he cannot obtain it.
>
> He may enter into the other, but that is the end of his kingdom; he cannot have an increase. (D&C 131:1–4)

We learn further of the highest degree.

> Therefore, when they are out of the world they neither marry nor are given in marriage; but are appointed angels in heaven, which angels are ministering servants, to minister for those who are worthy of a far more, and an exceeding, and an eternal weight of glory.
>
> For these angels did not abide my law; therefore, they cannot be enlarged, but remain separately and singly, without exaltation, in their saved condition, to all eternity; and from henceforth are not gods, but are angels of God forever and ever. (D&C 132:16–17)

Those who were denied the blessing of eternal marriage through no fault of their own, or because they lived in a day and age when such ordinances were not available, will not be denied the blessing of exaltation, for many such things will be reconciled during the Millennium. But, for others, the words of Alma are appropriate, for procrastination is a deadly enemy:

> For behold, this life is the time for men to prepare to
> meet God; yea, behold the day of this life is the day for men
> to perform their labors. (Alma 34:32)

~ ~ ~

What a grand reunion we will have when we finally return to our heavenly home and are embraced in the loving arms of Father and Mother, the King and Queen of Heaven. And can we imagine the greeting of our elder brother, Jesus, he who sacrificed so much in our behalf and worked so hard to guide us home? How the tears will flow! And how wonderful when we finally clasp in an embrace of love our earthly parents, spouses, and children. We will also greet relatives from all generations of time whom we have yet to become acquainted with. The veil which covered our eyes during our mortal probation will also be removed and we will once again recognize our former associations in the spirit world. Oh, what a happy reunion.

~ ~ ~

Because those who merit an inheritance in the Celestial Kingdom will be privileged to enjoy the association of both the Father and the Son, the earth must be prepared and made ready for their presence. Brigham Young teaches us that:

> When the earth is sanctified from the effects of the
> fall, and baptized, cleansed and purified by fire, and returns
> to its paradisiacal state, and has become like a sea of glass,
> as Urim and Thumim; when all this is done, and the Savior
> has presented the earth to his Father, and it is placed in the
> cluster of the celestial Kingdoms, and the Son and all his
> faithful brethren and sisters have received the welcome
> plaudit, "enter ye into the joy of your Lord," and the Savior
> is crowned, then, and not till then, will the Saints receive
> their everlasting inheritances.[4]

A white stone will then be given those who inherit a celestial reward.

Then the white stone mentioned in Revelations 2:17, will become a Urim and Thummim to each individual who receives one, whereby, things pertaining to a higher order of kingdoms will be made known;

And a white stone is given to each of those who come into the Celestial Kingdom, whereon is a new name written, which no man knoweth save he that receiveth it. The new name is the key word. (D&C 130:10–11)

The new celestialized world will be governed by a heavenly Jerusalem, which will be so magnificent that mortal man cannot begin to imagine it. Travel through the visions of John who recorded the nature of that glorious city.

And he carried me away in the spirit to a great and high mountain and shewed me that great city, the holy Jerusalem, descending out of heaven from God.

Having the glory of God: and her light was like unto a stone most precious, even like a jasper stone, clear as crystal;

And had a wall great and high, and had twelve gates, and at the gates twelve angels, and names written thereon, which are the names of the twelve tribes of the children of Israel;

On the east three gates; on the north three gates; on the south three gates; and on the west three gates.

And the wall of the city had twelve foundations, and in them the names of the twelve apostles of the Lamb.

And he that talked with me had a golden reed to measure the city, and the gates thereof, and the wall thereof.

And the city lieth foursquare, and the length is as large as the breadth; and he measured the city with the reed, twelve thousand furlongs. The length and the breadth and the height of it are equal.

And he measured the wall thereof, an hundred and forty and four cubits, according to the measure of a man, that is, of the angel.

And the building of the wall of it was of jasper; and the city was pure gold, like unto clear glass.

> And the foundations of the wall of the city were gar-
> nished with all manner of precious stones. The first founda-
> tion was jasper; the second, sapphire; the third, a chalcedony;
> the fourth, an emerald;
>
> The fifth, sardonyx; the seventh, chrysolite; the eight,
> beryl; the ninth, a topaz; the tenth, a chrysoprasus; the
> eleventh, a jacinth; the twelfth, an amethyst.
>
> And the twelve gates were twelve pearls; every sev-
> eral gate was of one pearl; and the street of the city as pure
> gold, as it were transparent glass.
>
> And I saw no temple therein; for the Lord God Almighty
> and the Lamb are the temple of it.
>
> And the city had no need of the sun, neither of the
> moon, to shine in it; for the glory of God did lighten it, and
> the Lamb is the light thereof. (Rev. 21:10–23)

How can we as mortal men envision a city whose length
and breadth and height are the same; a cube which measures
twelve thousand furlongs; a city of pure gold. The foundation
of the great wall surrounding the city and its gates will be
adorned with precious stones and the streets paved with gold
as clear as glass. It is no wonder so many descriptions of the
celestial kingdom describe it as a place of burnings.

~ ~ ~

The hearts of the saints yearn for a celestial reward, yet
so many doubt their qualifications for such a gift. Because the
flesh is weak and the trials of life weigh heavily upon our
shoulders we cannot help but feel inadequate and unworthy.
But, read the comforting words of Nephi on this subject.

> For the gate by which ye should enter is repentance
> and baptism by water; and then cometh a remission of your
> sins by fire and by the Holy Ghost.
>
> And then are ye in this strait and narrow path which
> leads to eternal life; yea, ye have entered in by the gate; ye
> have done according to the commandments of the Father
> and the Son; and ye have received the Holy Ghost, which

witnesses of the Father and the Son, unto the fulfilling of the promise which he hath made, that if ye entered in by the way ye should receive.

And now, my beloved brethren, after ye have gotten into this strait and narrow path, I would ask if all is done? Behold, I say unto you, Nay; for ye have not come thus far save it were by the word of Christ with unshaken faith in him, relying wholly upon the merits of him who is mighty to save.

Wherefore, ye must press forward with a steadfastness in Christ, having a perfect brightness of hope, and a love of God and of all men, wherefore, if ye shall press forward feasting upon the word of Christ, and endure to the end behold, thus saith the Father: Ye shall have eternal life. (2 Ne. 31:17–20)

What greater testimony do we need than this. *All who remain faithful and endure to the end will have eternal life!* Can we doubt those words when we fall victim to depression and weary of the fight? These are the very words that should propel us onward and upward in our struggles toward eternity.

Bruce R. McConkie also remarks on this subject.

Everyone who is on the straight and narrow path, who is striving and struggling and desiring to do what is right, though far from perfect in this life; if he passes out of this life while he's on the straight and narrow, he's going to go on to an eternal reward in his father's kingdom.

You don't need to get a complex or get a feeling, that you have to be perfect to be saved. You don't. There's only been one perfect person, and that's the Lord Jesus, but in order to be saved in the Kingdom of God and in order to pass the test of mortality, what you have to do is get on the straight and narrow path—thus charting a course leading to eternal life—and then, being on that path pass out of this life in full fellowship. I'm not saying that you don't have to keep the commandments. I'm saying you don't have to be perfect to be saved. The way it operates is this: you get on the path that's named the "straight and narrow." You do it by entering the gate of repentance and baptism. The straight and narrow path leads from the gate of repentance and baptism, a very great distance, to a reward that's called eternal life. If you're on that path and pressing forward, and you die, you'll never get off the path. There is no such thing as falling off the straight and narrow path in the life to come, and the reason is that this life is the time that is given to men to prepare for eternity. Now is the time and the day of your salvation, so if you're working zealously in this life— though you haven't done all you hoped you might do— you're still going to be saved. You don't have to do what Jacob said, "Go beyond the mark." You don't have to live a life that's truer than true, you don't have to have an excessive zeal that becomes fanatical and unbalancing. What you have to do is stay in the mainstream of the Church and live as upright and decent people in the Church—keeping the commandments, paying your tithing, serving in the organizations of the Church, loving the Lord, staying on the straight and narrow path. If you're on that path when death comes—because this is the time and day appointed, this is the probationary estate—you'll never fall off from it, and, for all practical purposes, your calling and election is made sure.[5]

Elder McConkie continues to teach us this principle:

We do not work out our salvation in a moment; it doesn't come to us in an instant, suddenly. Gaining salvation is a process. . . . We say that a man has to be born again, meaning that he has to die as pertaining to the unrighteous things in the world. . . . We are born again when we die as pertaining to unrighteousness and when we live as pertaining to the things of the spirit. But that doesn't happen in an instant, suddenly, that also is a process. Being born again is a gradual thing. . . .

So it is with the plan of salvation. We have to become perfect to be saved in the Celestial Kingdom. But nobody becomes perfect in this life. Only the Lord Jesus attained that state, and he had an advantage that none of us has. . . . But we must become perfect to gain a celestial inheritance. As it is with being born again, and as it is with sanctifying our souls, so becoming perfect in Christ is a process. . . .

As members of the Church, if we chart a course leading to eternal life; if we begin the processes of spiritual rebirth, and are going in the right direction; if we chart a course of sanctifying our souls, and degree by degree are going in that direction; and if we chart a course of becoming perfect, and, step by step and phase by phase, are perfecting our souls by overcoming the world, then it is absolutely guaranteed—there is no question whatever about it—we shall gain eternal life. Even though we have spiritual rebirth ahead of us, perfection ahead of us, the full degree of sanctification ahead of us, if we chart a course and follow it to the best of our ability in this life, then when we go out of this life we'll continue in exactly that same course. We'll no longer be subject to the passions and the appetites of the flesh. We will have passed successfully the tests of this mortal probation and in due course we'll get the fullness of our Father's Kingdom—and that means eternal life in his everlasting presence.

The prophet told us that there are many things that people have to do, even after the grave, to work out their salvation. We're not going to be perfect the minute we die. But if we've charted a course, if our desires are right, if our appetites are curtailed and bridled, and if we believe in the Lord and are doing to the very best of our abilities what we ought to do, we'll go on to everlasting salvation, which is the fullness of eternal reward in our Father's Kingdom. I think we ought to have hope; I think we ought to have rejoicing.[6]

We learn the gospel precept upon precept in much the same way we learn to walk step by step. Likewise, we perfect ourselves through trial and error—sometimes falling flat on our backs and other times soaring through the valleys of success. We also learn obedience through prayer and sacrifice, making our way up the ladder toward heaven one rung at a time. Thus, if our hearts are pure and our integrity unquestioned, if we love God and obey his counsel, if we are obedient to the command to be baptized and then receive the Holy Ghost, if we take upon ourselves the saving ordinances of the temple and honor those covenants made there, if we struggle to live the best we can, continuing steadfast until our mortal eyes close in sleep for the last time, our exaltation is assured. Thus, those who are obedient in this life and endure to the end, will ultimately find their rewards in the highest kingdom of heaven. The challenge then, is this life! It is while in the flesh that we decide whether to set our feet on a path which leads toward life eternal or whether to die in our sins.

No one will attain perfection in this life. Only the Savior held that distinction. Neither will we find perfection the moment we die, for there is still much to do on the other side. We must continue gaining knowledge not yet given, partaking of ordinances not yet available, and being endowed with powers and glories, one upon the other, until, at long last, we become recipients of exaltation. The path is clear. Hang on and let endurance be the key. Those who do so will one day look back upon this puny existence and will fully understand that everything they endured during their lifetime gave them experience and prepared them for their ultimate glory in the kingdom of God.

> They are they unto whose hands the Father has given all things—
>
> They are they who are priests and kings, who have received of his fullness, and of his glory;
>
> And are priests of the Most High, after the order of Melchizedek, which was after the order of Enoch, which was after the order of the Only Begotten Son.
>
> Wherefore, as it is written they are gods, even the sons of God. (D&C 76:55–58)

Let your hearts rejoice and praise God day and night for the plan of salvation and for the blessings which await the faithful. Rejoice that God loved us so much that those who believe in him and remain true to their covenants will enjoy his companionship in the Celestial Kingdom. The glories which await the faithful are so grand and so magnificent that words cannot express them, yet the promise is fixed for those who endure well. Thus, we must lift up our hearts and praise God continually for his mercy and for those blessings he will ultimately pour down upon the faithful.

~ ~ ~

Notes

1. Brigham Young, *Journal of Discourses*, 6:282
2. Brigham Young, *Journal of Discourses,* 9:148.
3. Ibid., 7:163.
4. Ibid., 17:117.
5. McConkie, "Probationary Test," 11.
6. Millett and McConkie, *Life Beyond,* 138–39.

Chapter Twelve

Enduring to the End

And again, be patient in tribulation until I come;
and, behold I come quickly, and my reward is with me,
and they who have sought me early shall find rest to
their souls. Even so Amen. (D&C 54:10)

One of the greatest challenges of man is to endure to the end. The expectations of the Millennium or of celestial glories will have no meaning if we fall short of the mark and succumb to the forces of evil. If, at the close of our mortal probation we have allowed Satan to steal away our hearts, we will lose the reward of the faithful, for only those who serve God and endure to the end will continue on to exaltation. Now, this in no way means that we must be perfect in this life for only the Savior attained that state, but we must remain steadfast and submissive and bow to the will of the Father in all things if we are to counted worthy of so great a blessing.

When our sojourn on this earth comes to an end, the righteous will enter a state of happiness where the frailties of mortality are passed away. Our probationary state will everlastingly be finished at this point, and we will no longer be subjected to pain and discouragement or with bouts of anger or depression. Those who choose to follow God and embrace the light will now find all the enlightenment their hearts desire, and, with the weaknesses of the flesh gone, will climb upward and onward until they make their way home to God. All too often, however, we find ourselves sinking in the mire of discouragement Satan places in our path to keep us down. He clogs our minds with despair and muddies the waters of reason until he carefully leads us into mists of confusion. Thus, we must be ever alert and fight a battle as never before to maintain a strong foothold on the path of truth and a firm grip on the Iron Rod.

Unfortunately, the natural forces of life and the unrighteousness of so many often place a heavy burden on us and we question why a loving God permits such unhappiness. We search and pray and often find no relief. Thus, our hearts turn cold and indifferent and soon the spirit can no longer find entrance. How sad this is, for evil warriors are just waiting to seize upon such moments that they might carefully lead us into the realms of darkness and capture our souls. Therefore, we must be ever cautious of those who wish to weaken our will.

Even though there are times when we seek for heavenly comfort and seem to search in vain, be not deceived in this observation, for God has us firmly in view and knows what is needed before we ask. He wraps his mighty cloak of protection around us in ways seldom understood, and buoys us up and succors our needs even when we think not. Our prayers are always heard by the courts on high and truly we are never left to ourselves.

Part of our mission in life is to overcome all things; to endure until we think we cannot endure more; to struggle until we lie panting on the floor; to stretch and grow beyond our abilities until, at long last, the physical body matches more closely the noble state of our spirits. God's time and our time are not always the same, however, and those strengths and blessings that we search for may not come until the body has been tempered and refined and has become a proper repository for them.

As hard as life is, we should try to set aside our forebodings and be a happy people. We of all people should glory in this life, for we understand so much concerning salvation and just what awaits the faithful in the mansions on high. Thus, our hearts should leap for joy, and we should gain happiness from even the simple pleasures of life and enjoy the warm companionship of our children, spouses, parents, and friends.

God is good to us. He has blessed us beyond measure and has given us a beautiful world to enjoy. He has placed music at our fingertips and created voices and melodies to fill the air. He has placed us in circumstances which best suit our needs and governs the affairs of our growth and schooling personally. He lends an ear when trials appear and often softens a hurt, opens a door, or soothes a brow when no one else on earth can do it. He is there at our invitation through prayer, and his understanding of our needs is unquestioned. He created a mind that can seek the wonders of the universe, an eye that can see roses, and a hand that can rock the cradle of love. Attributes which, if directed wisely, can bring untold happiness and joy. Thus, blessings rain steadily upon the righteous and we ere in our inclination to lash out and deny God's goodness. Therefore, we must be patient in our afflictions and continue onward and upward toward that light which leads to life eternal.

So often we are able to look back on a period of time when we felt that we were alone, and then later, with a broader view of things, could readily see the hand of God in the outcome of those events which troubled us so deeply at the time. Unfortunately, our finite minds are limited in their abilities to discern the things of God. Therefore, we must learn to trust in his word and remember that he is directing the affairs of mankind and has not, nor will ever, forsake us.

Blessings come by obedience to those principles upon which they are predicated. If we willfully disregard a natural law, we must expect to reap the consequences. All too often, however, the innocent are at the mercy of others who break the law and thus must often endure the same consequences or feel the same pain. It is during these bleak times that we must pray and trust that he will give us added strength to endure our heartaches.

Sadly, tribulation, stress, persecution and despair are the common lot of man. Moreover, Lucifer is waging all out war not only on the saints but on all men everywhere. Our society is so filled with corruption that its wicked influence greets us at every turn. It seems that every aspect of our lives is somehow touched by the controlling hands of despicable men and women. Often our financial well being, our health needs, our hope for a secure future, and even our freedoms and God-given rights seem to be at the mercy of forces outside of our control. Portions of our democratic system of government have been warped and twisted over the years, causing injustices of such magnitude that many have begun to rebel against their neighbors, cities, and states.

So often we pray and search the scriptures for answers to those difficult places in our lives, but all too often it seems the heavens are closed to us. The soul wrenching cry to the Lord, God Almighty during the imprisonment of Joseph Smith in Liberty Jail could well be the cry of many of us in these troubling times.

> O God, where art thou? and where is the pavilion that covereth thy hiding place?
>
> How long shall thy hand be stayed, and thine eye, yea thy pure eye, behold from the eternal heavens the wrongs of thy people and of thy servants, and thine ear be penetrated with their cries?
>
> Yea, O Lord, how long shall they suffer these wrongs and unlawful oppression, before thine heart shall be softened toward them, and thy bowels be moved with compassion toward them?
>
> O Lord God Almighty, maker of heaven, earth, and seas, and of all things that in them are, and who controllest and subjectest the devil, and the dark and benighted dominion of Sheol—stretch forth thy hand; let thine eye pierce; let thy pavilion be taken up; let thy hiding place no longer be cov-

ered; let thine ear be inclined; let thine heart be softened, and thy bowels moved with compassion toward us.

Let thine anger be kindled against our enemies; and, in the fury of thine heart, with thy sword avenge us of our wrongs.

Remember thy suffering saints, O our God; and thy servants will rejoice in thy name forever. (D&C 121:1–6)

Our trials also seem overwhelming at times and cannot always be dismissed easily. Financial reversals of every kind seem to plague the families of today sending them into angry bouts of depression. Sickness and disease are rampant among us and there are few who escape. A new form of restlessness has crept into the hearts of our young people and many go astray. Taxes seem to exceed our income and insurance demands keep going up. Liability expenses of every kind drain our pocket-books and unsavory characters lurk in the shadows to deceive us and to relieve us of our possessions and security.

Often we search desperately for some measure of that self esteem that was so cruelly ripped away by divorce, child abuse, or the violence so symptomatic of our decaying society. Our daily trials seem so great at times we sometimes find ourselves overwhelmed with discouragement. Why is my child sick? Why did we lose our job? Why can't we get ahead? Why does the car keep breaking? Why am I not loved? Why aren't my efforts appreciated? Why must I endure such pain? Why must there be war? Why did we loose our home? Why the tornado, hurricane, or flood? Why the death that ripped away our hearts? Why so many injustices when we are trying so hard to live in accordance to the commands of the Lord? Why has he forsaken us? Why can't we have a miracle in our lives? Why must we endure so much? Haven't we had enough? These and more keep us from the joy that we all search for, and often threaten our testimonies and thus jeopardize our salvation.

Unfortunately, Lucifer sits in the wings and waits for the opportunity to lure us away with answers that please the mind but ultimately lead us down to hell. Listen to the answer of our God to the plea's of his servant Joseph and draw strength from his word and from the promises of tomorrow.

> My son, peace be unto thy soul; thine adversity and thine afflictions shall be but a small moment;
>
> And then if thou endure it well, God shall exalt thee on high; thou shalt triumph over all thy foes.
>
> Thy friends do stand by thee, and they shall hail thee again with warm hearts and friendly hands.
>
> Thou art not yet as Job; thy friends do not contend against thee, neither charge thee with transgression, as they did Job.
>
> And they who do charge thee with transgression, their hope shall be blasted, and their prospects shall melt away as the hoar frost melteth before the burning rays of the rising sun; . . .
>
> Wo unto all those that discomfort my people, and drive, and murder, and testify against them, saith the Lord of Hosts; a generation of vipers shall not escape the damnation of hell.
>
> Behold, mine eyes see and know all their works, and I have in reserve a swift judgment in the season thereof, for them all.
>
> For there is a time appointed for every man, according as his works shall be. (D&C 121:7–11, 23–25)

The afflictions of the early saints were of such magnitude that they prayed day and night for deliverance. Joseph questioned the Lord about the necessity for so much tribulation and pain. After conversing with the Lord he makes this impressive observation concerning the trials which had come upon so many:

> I know that Zion, in due time of the Lord, will be redeemed; but how many will be the days of her purification, tribulation, and affliction, the Lord has kept hid from my eyes; and when I inquire concerning this subject the voice of the Lord is: "Be still, and know that I am God! All those who suffer for my name shall reign with me, and he that layeth down his life for my sake shall find it again."[1]

The Lord's further council is sobering:

> If thou art called to pass through tribulation; if thou art in perils among false brethren; if thou art in perils among robbers; if thou art in perils by land or by sea;
>
> If thou art accused with all manner of false accusations; if thine enemies fall upon thee; if they tear thee from the society of thy father and mother and brethren and sisters; and if with a drawn sword thine enemies tear thee from the bosom of thy wife, and of thine offspring, and thine elder son, although but six years of age, shall cling to thy garments, and shall say, My father, my father, why can't you stay with us? O, my father, what are the men going to do with you and if then he shall be thrust from thee by the sword, and thou be dragged to prison, and thine enemies prowl around thee like wolves for the blood of the lamb;
>
> And if thou shouldst be cast into the pit, or into the hands of murderers, and the sentence of death passed upon thee; if thou be cast into the deep; if the billowing surge conspire against thee; if fierce winds become thine enemy; if the heavens gather blackness, and all the elements combine to hedge up the way; and above all, if the very jaws of hell shall gape open the mouth wide after thee, know thou, my son, that all these things shall give thee experience, and shall be for they good. (D&C 122:5–7)

How much plainer could the scriptures be on the subject of experience? This sojourn in mortality is but a moment in the expanse of eternity. The time is so very short and there is so much to learn to become worthy candidates for celestial living.

All people everywhere earn their rewards by the use of their agency and by struggling with the forces of good and evil. God in his wisdom has ordained that we learn obedience by experience and suffering. Thus, we cannot know the good without the bad. Nor can we learn of joy without experiencing the awful depths of sorrow. We simply cannot become perfect without purifying ourselves through every trial and every ordeal that God has outlined for our benefit.

The prophet Joseph Smith gives us further insights into

the matter of tribulation in his teachings.

> It is a shame for the Saints to talk of chastisement, and transgressions, when all the Saints before them, prophets and apostles, have had to come up through great tribulation; whether a Herod, a Nero, or a Boggs, causes the affliction, or the blood to be shed, is all the same,—these murderers will have their reward! and the saints theirs. How many have had to wander in sheep skins and goat skins, and live in caves and dens of the mountains, because the world was unworthy of their society! And was transgression or chastisement connected with their seclusion from the enjoyment of society? No! But remember, brethren, he that offends one of the least of the Saints, would be better off with a mill stone tied to his neck and he and the stone plunged into the depth of the sea![2]

There seems to be a need for the mortal tabernacle to endure suffering. To have miracles working daily in our lives proves only to our physical senses that God lives. Unfortunately, the physical senses are often weak. Thus, it is the spirit that holds the strength to see us through hard times and it is the spirit that must be strengthened.

Faith is the power which propels us upward toward the light of Christ and into the presence of God. It is the proving ground and the means whereby all things are acted upon. Men who are converted by miracles alone are only converted physically, for it is the eye which beheld the miracle. Yes, it burns our bosoms and causes serious reflection and change to come upon us, but such revelations are of short duration, for the memory of the physical fades all too quickly from our minds. The spirit, on the other hand, has power to change men's hearts and change his direction from a life of sin to one of righteousness. It is the spirit which communes with God. It is for this reason the Holy Ghost remains in his spirit form, that he, as spirit, might commune with the spirits of men in mortality and bring them to the knowledge of their Creator.

God must have a tried people. It must be that they struggle and pray daily for their needs and wants until they recognize, at long last, that they are indebted to God for even the air they breath. They must learn that all blessings come from God. He is the Creator and owns all things and if we are to enjoy any blessing it must come from him. He, like any parent, wishes us to ask and to acknowledge his hand in the gifts that we receive. Moreover, he wishes us to give thanks for those gifts already given. He wishes us to understand that he is in control of all things and wishes us to humble ourselves before him and be submissive to his will. He wishes us to love him and to honor his name through righteous behavior, that he might then in turn bless us with the treasures of heaven.

Often the lessons he chooses for us are hard and we suffer immeasurably. Unfortunately, most of us fail to understand the principles of experience and suffering.

> And now, beloved brethren, we say unto you, that inasmuch as God hath said that He would have a tried people, that He would purge them as gold, now we think that this time He has chosen His own crucible, wherein we have been tried; and we think if we get through with any degree of safety, and shall have kept the faith, that it will be a sign to this generation, altogether sufficient to leave them without excuse; and we think also, it will be a trial of our faith equal to that of Abraham, and that the ancients will not have whereof to boast over us in the day of judgment, as being called to pass through heavier afflictions; that we may hold an even weight in the balance with them; but now, after having suffered so great sacrifice and having passed though so great a season of sorrow, we trust that a ram may be caught in the thicket speedily, to relieve the sons and daughters of Abraham from their great anxiety, and to light up the lamp of salvation upon their countenances, that they may hold on now, after having gone so far unto everlasting life.[3]

Thus, it is absolutely necessary for us to be tried—to see if we blaspheme God when times are hard or whether we remain true and faithful and walk by faith, knowing that God is purifying the metal of each of us. The refiners fire causes pain of both body and soul. Nonetheless, we must be willing to be tried and tempered and molded into vessels worthy to house the Spirit of God.

~ ~ ~

As strange as it may seem, adversity deals with love. If we get no other thought clear in our minds, it must be the truth of the great and infinite love the Father has for his children. Every trial, every lesson, every cause for mourning or suffering is part of a divinely orchestrated plan for our perfection.

We, as parents, watch as our toddlers begin to take their first steps and quickly catch them when they fall. Nonetheless, we have visions of the time when that child will be running and playing and being carried through the seasons of life on two strong, bold legs. We smile at that baby who looks so trustingly into our eyes, and then we take a few steps back and encourage the child to walk alone. His eyes question why we have moved; why the security of our arms are no longer there. He may even cry. But in our wisdom and because of our great love for him we maintain our distance, and, looking down we lovingly say, "No, little one, it is you who must come to me."

Each new phase of that child's life will follow much the same pattern. Each new experience he encounters will teach him to share, to serve and to love. We as parents must teach him both by word and example; teaching too, by chastisement and discipline; carefully molding, nurturing and refining each trait until the refinement of character produces, at last, a self motivating adult.

Now magnify this principle by eternal standards and consider a Father in Heaven who is concerned not only for our mortal bodies but for that spirit that he had already nurtured for eons of time; a spirit child who was schooled at his knee long before we took upon ourselves a tabernacle of flesh; a spirit who learned and mastered a variety of talents and developed varying degrees of character, all of which would one day enhance its mortal experience.

We, as the children of the Father, have come so far. We shouted for joy at the grand council as the plan for our salvation was laid out before us. We watched as the earth was prepared, as loved ones moved forward and as history rolled on before us. We continued to grow and to perfect ourselves in that spirit state until we were worthy to stand before the priesthood in preparation for our sojourn on earth, and, with hands laid upon our heads, received a great blessing: a "calling and election," to move through the portals of life as members of the Abrahamic line and to be heirs of all the blessings promised that great patriarch and his lineage. But, our greatest task now lay ahead of us, to make that call and election *sure*—that state of being that would assure us entrance into the Celestial Kingdom where the valiant will enjoy the association of the Father and Son and receive of those magnificent blessings that come from being in their presence.

As we struggle through mortality and search the heavens for further light and knowledge concerning our mortal schooling, the path becomes clear. Through diligence and study we soon learn that the tests and trials, the tempering and refinement, the stretching and growing, are all for one purpose—to perfect us to the degree that we might have our *"call and election made sure,"* for this glorious blessing will come only after the trial of our faith and allows us entrance into that inner circle of those who are members of the Church of the First Born.

Those who partake of the saving ordinances of the gospel and who make holy covenants are those that are candidates for such great blessings. Thus, the path is narrow. Only those who endure all things and endure them well, who are determined to serve God and their fellow man at all costs, who endure the trials of life and through suffering and despair still love, still serve and still cling to the Iron Rod will have their call and election made sure. These are they who are entitled to the Second Comforter; the ministering of the Savior himself. What a blessing to strive for, to endure for, and to sacrifice for.

This, then, is the Father's ultimate goal for us. His work and his glory is to bring his sons and daughters home to that inner circle, and his greatest joy will be realized when, at long last, he is able to gather the righteous about him. The veil which clouded our view for so long will then be dropped, and our understanding enlarged to grasp the magnitude of the Father's love—that divine love which we doubted at times when he stood back and said, "No, my little one, it is you who must come to me."

When viewed from an eternal perspective, adversity then takes on a new meaning, and love becomes the grand key. It was his infinite love for us that brought our spirits into existence and then nurtured them for untold periods of time. It was through the power of his love that a plan was designed for our salvation; a plan that, through righteousness, would ultimately bring us to a fullness of joy and happiness.

This plan would take us from the security of our pre-mortal world and into the mists of forgetfulness where we could be tried and tested and where we could prove ourselves worthy of exaltation. Mortality would be our last and greatest challenge but with it would also come our greatest rewards.

The great Elohim holds many titles but the most precious to him is that of Father. He watches over his little flock with great love and care. Though the road seems hard and the path often darkened by despair, we are never alone. The Father loves us beyond our ability to comprehend and it is precisely because of this love for us that he carefully moves back a step or two during our mortal probation and allows us time to flounder and fall and to gain strength and to make our way, inch by inch, toward eternal goals.

During those times of floundering in the mire of mortality, we sometimes question the path he has chosen for us. Often we suffer great tribulation and are pained by the trials of life and often we search for him and find him not. When things seem their bleakest we cry out, "where art thou?"—and often we find no answer! But our great Father God stands near and fights back his tender feelings and desires to shield us from pain and stays his mighty hand time after time, that we might learn to walk by faith and develop inner strength; that in doing so we might stretch beyond our reach and lengthen our stride and, thus, learn those lessons of humility, love, patience and sacrifice that could be learned in no other way.

It is only by this stretching and growing that our mortal characters will become refined into celestial characters. It is only through trials and struggles that our weaknesses will become our strengths and it is only by enduring in faith and submitting to the will of the Father that these strengths can then sustain us through this life and on into eternity.

If each time we are sick we were instantly healed we would not learn of suffering, patience or service to one another. If we never had financial reversals we would not learn humility and dependence upon the Lord. If we were never asked to care for a child or an elderly parent or some other afflicted soul, we might never find cause to reach into the depths of our soul for that patience and long suffering that so often lies dormant within us. When we pray for strength or patience or any other worthwhile quality, the Lord does not immediately shower that gift upon us but instead throws in our path a series of experiences which enables us to develop that quality ourselves.

Just as talents come to us as gifts yet remain undeveloped until we struggle through study and practice to develop them, so also are the qualities of character and personality developed. We develop them through experience, by trial and error and through study and prayer. Thus, if we lack charity we must work to love and serve. If we desire patience we must practice patience. If we desire knowledge we must study, read and work toward that end, for nothing worth having was ever had easily. Neither is the gift of eternal life given easily, but comes to us only after a lifetime of service to one's fellow man and by obedience to those laws God has given us.

Life is an adventure. We were placed in our earthly circumstance by the merits of our premortal existence. Likewise, we will be honored in our heavenly home by the merits and works achieved in this life. Thus, it is through the struggles of mortality that we prepare ourselves for the blessings of eternity. Each time we master a fault, or strengthen a virtue, we come closer to perfection and to the glorious blessings of exaltation and become candidates for celestial living. The road is not an easy one, however, and each of us must struggle toward perfection step by step. We must dig deep and weed out the bad and then nurture the good within us until we reach that point where God will know that he can trust us and that we will do nothing that is contrary to his holy mind and will.

As the little child stumbles and falls and slowly learns to walk, and then by practice learns to skip and run and jump, so must our eternal characters be developed, here a little, there a little, until we develop qualities of love and charity, service and patience, mastery of self, intellect, and all the traits necessary to transform us into a celestial being.

Brigham Young teaches us:

> Trials are necessary—we are now in a day of trial to prove ourselves worthy or unworthy of the life which is to come.[4]

He continues:

> All intelligent beings who are crowned with crowns of glory, immortality and eternal lives must pass through every ordeal appointed for intelligent beings to pass through, to gain their glory and exaltation. Every calamity that can come upon mortal beings will be suffered to come upon the few, to prepare them to enjoy the presence of the Lord. If we obtain the glory that Abraham obtained, we must do so by the same means that he did. If we are ever prepared to enjoy the society of Enoch, Noah, Melchizedek, Abraham, Isaac, and Jacob, or of their faithful children and of the faith-

ful prophets and apostles, we must pass through the same experience and gain the knowledge, intelligence and endowments that will prepare us to enter into the Celestial Kingdom of our Father and God. How many of the Latter-day saints will endure all these things, and be prepared to enjoy the presence of the Father and the Son? You can answer that question at your leisure. Every trial and experience you have passed through is necessary for your salvation.[5]

Brigham Young understood the principles of persecution and trials so well that he was able to exclaim:

Well, do you think that persecution has done us good? Yes. I sit and laugh, and rejoice exceedingly when I see persecution. I care no more about it than I do about the whistling of the north wind, the croaking of the crane that flies over my head, or the cracking of the thorn under the pot. The Lord has all things in his hand; therefore let it come, for it will give me experience.[6]

Thus, we must endure our trials and tribulations patiently, calling upon God the Father of us all for consolation, peace and the strength necessary to enable us to endure to the end and enjoy all that the Father has promised us. Those who do so and who live through the last times when the earth is ultimately cleansed and transformed into a terrestrial sphere, will enjoy the companionship of the Savior in the great day of the Millennium and will enjoy untold happiness and joy.

~ ~ ~

Notes

1. Smith, *History of the Church,* 1:453–54.
2. Smith, *Teachings of the Prophet,* 260.
3. Ibid., 136.
4. Brigham Young, *Journal of Discourses,* 12:167.
5. Ibid., 8:150.
6. Ibid., 2:8.

Bibliography

Andrus, Hyrum L. *Doctrines of the Kingdom.* Foundations of the Millenial Kingdom of Christ, vol. 3. Salt Lake City: Bookcraft, 1973.

Conference Report. April 6, 1837.

Journal History of the Church. Church Archives, The Church of Jesus Christ of Latter-day Saints, Salt Lake City, microfilm copy in Harold B. Lee Library, Brigham Young University, Provo, Utah.

Journal of Discourses. 26 vols. Liverpool: F. D. Richards, 1855–86.

Lee, Harold B., *Conference Report*, April 1943.

Lee, Harold B. *Improvement Era* (June 1948): 320.

Lund, Gerald N. *The Coming of the Lord.* Salt Lake City: Bookcraft, 1971.

McConkie, Bruce R. "Stand Independent above All Other Creatures." *Ensign* 9 (May 1979): 92-94.

McConkie, Bruce R. "The Probationary Test of Mortality." Talk given at University of Utah Institute of Religion, January 10, 1982. Found in: Yorgenson, Blaine M. & Brent G., *Spiritual Survival in the Last Days*, 268-270. Deseret Book, Salt Lake City, Utah, 1990.

McConkie, Bruce R. *The Millennial Messiah: The Second Coming of the Son of Man.* Salt Lake City: Deseret Book, 1982.

McKinlay, Lynn A. *Life Eternal: A Series of Four Lectures Delivered to the Young People's Temple Group of the South Davis Stake.* Salt Lake City: Deseret Book, 1950.

Millet, Robert L., and Joseph Fielding McConkie. *The Life Beyond.* Salt Lake City: Bookcraft, 1986.

Penrose, Charles W. "The Second Advent." *Millennial Star* 21 (September 10, 1859): 583.

Pratt, Orson. *Equality and Oneness of the Saints.*

Pratt, Parley P. *Key to the Science of Theology,* Deseret Book Company, Salt Lake City, Utah, 1973.

Pratt, Parley P., Jr., ed. *The Autobiography of Parley P. Pratt.* 4th ed. Salt Lake City: Deseret Book, 1985.

Smith, Joseph, Jr. *Juvenile Instructor* 15 (May 1, 1880): 111.

Smith, Joseph, Jr. *History of The Church of Jesus Christ of Latter-day Saints.* Ed. B. H. Roberts. 2d ed., rev. 7 vols. Salt Lake City: Deseret Book, 1971.

Smith, Joseph Fielding, comp. *Teachings of the Prophet Joseph Smith.* Salt Lake City: Deseret Book, 1972.

Smith, Joseph Fielding. *Gospel Doctrine,* 442, Deseret Book Co., Salt Lake City, Utah, 1919.

Taylor, John. *The Government of God.* Liverpool, England: S. W. Richards, 1852.

Young, Brigham. *The Essential Brigham Young.* Classics in Mormon thought, vol. 3. Salt Lake City: Signature Books, 1992.